Dark Peak Aircraft Wrecks

(BOOK 2)

by
Ron Collier

Maps by Wes Hobson

ACCESS TO OPEN COUNTRY

Seventy Six square miles of the moorlands of the Peak District are open to the public through access agreements between the Peak National Park Joint Planning Board and the owners of the land, subject to certain conditions, the Board's byelaws and the closure on up to 12 days in the grouse shooting season (August 12th — December 10th.)

All the aircraft wrecks in this publication are on private land and permission is required from individual landowners to dig at these sites. If permission is not sought and a person is seen to be digging, an offence may have been committed under the Theft Act 1968 and that person could be summonsed under this Act (Maximum Penalty — £400 or 6 months imprisonment or both).

MINISTRY OF DEFENCE

Crashed United Kingdom military aircraft and their equipment remain the property of the Crown until such time as the M.O.D. decide to dispose of them.

Crashed enemy aircraft and their equipment lying within the U.K. are regarded as captured enemy property which has been surrended to the Crown.

Crashed American military aircraft remain the property of the United States Government, but the M.O.D. acts on behalf of the U.S. Authorities.

Any group wishing to recover the wreckage of military aircraft should first approach:- The M.O.D. Air Force Board Secretariat, Room 8239, Main Building, Whitehall, London SW1A 2HB.

Consent must be obtained with respect to each and every recovery operation and any failure will result in recovery becoming an unlawful interference with Crown property and could lead to Civil or Criminal proceedings.

Warning

The moors of the Peak District are mountains, and in bad weather, which can occur at any time, these moors can be dangerous. Adequate clothing plus map and compass should be carried at all times. It is advisable to inform someone of where you are going and stick to the intended route. For MOUNTAIN RESCUE ring: 999 or RIPLEY 43551 (POLICE OPERATIONS ROOM).

PHILLIP SHAW.
GLOSSOP
FEBRUARY 1981.

Published by Wharncliffe Woodmoor Ltd.
47 Church Street, Barnsley, South Yorkshire S70 2AS.

Case bound ISBN 0 950 7892 0 8
Paperback ISBN 0 950 7892 1 6

Printed by Joseph Ward & Co. Printers Ltd.
Dewsbury, West Yorkshire, WF13 1HR.

Photo overleaf BEA Dakota G-AHCY. Crashed at Wimberry Stones, Greenfield, 19th August, 1949, killing 24 of the 32 on board.

Contents

EARLY DAYS. Hampden L4055 7
NO MOUNT FOR AN ACE. Defiant N1766 12
TAIL END CHARLIE. Wellington W5719 22
SOUTH WEST BY NORTH EAST. Lysander V9403 28
MASTER BOMBER. Wellington DV810 32
BOUNCING BOMBER. Wellington X3348 36
ONE BROKEN JUG. Thunderbolt 416227 44
FLYING BOMB USN. PB4Y-1 63934 50
THE LOST SUMMER. Spitfire P7883 58
NIGHTFIGHTER VICTIM. Halifax HR727 63
FIRST AND LAST TIME. Stirling LJ628 75
ONE OF SIKORSKI'S TOURISTS. Anson N9853 82
OX BOX ON BROWN KNOLL. Oxford HN594 92
EVEN THE BEST. Oxford NM683 105
Anson N9912 112
Wellington R1011 113
Oxford LX518 114
Possible V1 site 116
Tiger Moth 117
Mustang P51D 118
Barracuda MD963 119
AEROBATIC FLYER. Meteor RA487 120
Consult TF-RPM 126
Vampire 127
Wellington MF627 128
Beaver L-20 26145 129
List of Dark Peak sites 130
Mountain Rescue 131
Ministry of Defence Guide to Recovery Groups 134

Without a doubt it was one of the most disastrous days that the RAF had experienced in peacetime. Seven twin-engined biplanes of 102 Squadron had set out from Aldergrove in Northern Ireland to return to their base at RAF Finningley on the morning of December 12th, 1936 — only one arrived safely.

The Handley Page Heyfords, each carrying a crew of four, had taken off at 10.45 in perfect weather conditions. Flying in loose V formation they crossed the Irish Sea passing over the English coast at Barrow-in-Furness, before them was a huge cloud mass of icy fog.

Fully expecting the clouds to disperse as they flew inland they pressed on into the 'clag'. Immediately ice began to form on the wings and control of the bombers became more difficult. Leading the formation, Squadron Leader Attwood was unable to keep the bombers together and each individual Heyford got swallowed up. From then on it became a struggle for every pilot to save himself and his crew.

For sometime the ungainly machines roared on looking for possible landing places while falling petrol gauges spelt danger to watchful pilots.

Sergeant Biddulph, after much difficulty, located Finningley and made a perfect landing through the murk. A worried reception committee awaited them. The sergeant pilot thought that he was in trouble for getting in late, and that he was the last plane down, when in fact he was the only one to arrive safely.

Six air dramas were being played out in different parts of the country as Biddulph taxied towards the hanger.

Sergeant Williams in Heyford K4864 crash-landed at Gainsborough . . . he and his crew were safely down. Heyford K5188 piloted by Flying Officer Gyll Murray force landed near York they too were unhurt. Squadron Leader Attwood in K4868 circled a field at Jackson Edge, Disley, close by the boundary of the Peak District. Keeping close to his leader was Pilot Officer Clifford in K6898.

Attwood brought of a perfect landing in the small field and the crew were able to watch as Clifford attempted a landing in the next field. On the second attempt Clifford's Heyford tore through some fencing, touched down, smashed through sets of iron railings, ripped up a telegraph pole and came to rest with its nose in a shrubbbery. The crew climbed out of the wreckage unhurt.

Nosing its way through the murk over Hebden Bridge was K6900 piloted by Sergeant Otter. The crew were peering down trying to get their bearings as the bomber skimmed the chimney pots. A mile from the town the machine struck a low wall and ploughed its way up a steep rutted hillside where it burst into flames killing three of the crew. Sergeant Otter escaped with his life.

K4874 was in difficulty over Oldham as it circled around for half an hour before crashing in the yard of Dingle Farm, at the northern edge of the Peak District.

Minutes before the crash Flight Lieutenant Pat Villiers had ordered his crew to jump. Then, with ice building up on the control surfaces, he trimmed the aircraft as

best he could, made his way down the fuselage to the lower mid-turret aperture and dropped out into the swirling mist. Apart from him breaking a leg upon landing, he and his crew got off lightly.

At the court of inquiry that followed pack ice forming on aircraft surfaces was blamed for the diaster. It was agreed that conditions like it had never been experienced before. Conditions experienced by pilots of 102 Squadron were to be encountered by many more pilots in the next decade as the war years brought about an increase in flying activity.

Over fifty aircraft crashed in the Dark Peak alone leaving wreckage that persists to this day.

The question is constantly being asked as to the probability of there being undiscovered aircraft on the moors. Whilst it is most unlikely there always remains the possibility. There are still areas of moorland that rarely see a hiker, rock climber, or gamekeeper — areas that are so laced with gulleys and bogs that no one would go there for pleasure. It is in these areas, far from the recognised paths, that an aircraft could remain undiscovered embedded deep in the peat.

In the late nineteen sixties a shepherd in the Highlands of Scotland noticed something sticking out of the ground. It turned out to be a Wellington bomber which had been given up for lost over the North Sea during the war. Although he had been in that particular area many times he had seen no sign of it before.

Flight Lieutenant Pat Villiers (above) ordered his crew to jump when they became completely lost in the cloud and fog over northern England. Heyford K4874, Villiers' aircraft about to enter the cloud bank that would bring down six of the bombers. Picture taken from another Heyford in the formation.

6 News of the World, DEC. 20, 1936

R.A.F. FLIGHT ENDS IN DISASTER

THREE MEN KILLED: FOUR ESCAPE BY PARACHUTE

SEVEN R.A.F. bombing machines left Aldergrove Aerodrome, Northern Ireland, the other day, to fly to Finningley, Yorkshire. Only one reached its destination.

Two crashed in flames; the others made forced landings in various parts of the country. Three men were killed in one crash; four others escaped by making parachute leaps a few moments before their machine swooped to destruction.

It was one of the most disastrous days the R.A.F. has ever known.

The seven machines, heavy night

BURNING MAN ON MOOR

Introduction

Wartime aviation history is recorded in the crash sites to be found in the Peak District National Park. Each pile of rusting metal to be found on the high ground represents a chapter in the air war waged against Germany.

From an early bombing raid to Europe by Hampdens of 83 Squadron, in the days before highly planned mass bomber operations, to every aspect of aircrew training. Twin-engined Oxfords of Advanced Flying Units, Wellingtons of Operational Training Units, a Stirling from a Heavy Conversion Unit. Later Bomber Command operations are represented by the Halifax returning with one engine shot up, damage sustained over Frankfurt.

A Spitfire on a training flight running out of fuel; a nightfighter of a type disliked by its crews, abandoned and left to crash on the hills above Derwent, represent Fighter Command.

American involvement is seen in the P47 Thunderbolt plucked out of the sky by a thunderstorm; a United States Navy PB4Y abandoned by its crew after being turned onto a course that would take it through central England — its bomb-bays heavy with depth charges.

Very few navigational aids, problems with radio's, over confidence, poor judgement, atrocious weather, enemy action and high ground all had a part to play. Some of the best pilots and navigators came to grief in the Peak District and survived to tell the tale. This work is an attempt to tell their stories which in the event, has resulted in a brief history of the air war from 1940 to 1945.

One of the 102 Sqd. Heyfords.

Photo via Air Vice Marshall Otter.

Hampden L4069 of 83 Squadron. SAYERS

Early Days

Hampden L4055 of 83 Squadron returning to Scampton after a raid on the German railway system in the area of Munchen-Gladbach, crashed near Holmfirth on May 23, 1940. Map reference 098058.

They were desperate days, the "phoney" war of the autumn and winter of '39 had ended with the invasion of Holland and Belgium in the spring of 1940. That initial surge of German forces into the lowlands of Europe had not been unexpected by the British and French — it took place on Friday, May 10th, 1940.

Allied counter-action for just such an attack called for an advance into Belgium to hold what they thought was the main German thrust into the north. When the British Expeditionary Force along with the cream of the French Army moved into Belgium, they had fallen into a trap.

Hitler's northern invasion was not the main attack. Army Group 'A' under Von Rundstedt, advanced through the wooded hills of the Ardennes and within eleven days had reached the Channel. The Allied forces were cut in two and the BEF was falling back on the Channel port of Dunkirk.

The French insisted on support from RAF Bomber Command, the British Army called for help against the mighty Blitzkrieg machine that was driving them backwards to the sea.

Supplies and communications were to be the target for the British bombers. On May 22nd, 1940, 28 airmen, the crews of seven Hampdens of 83 Squadron at Scampton, were briefed for a raid that night.

At the disposal of the advancing Germans was a vast railway network which was busy carrying supplies and reinforcements to the frontier. Although daylight raids were proving too costly in aircraft brought down by flak and fighters, night attacks on the rail communications could have some success.

Code names for attacks on rail and road transport was "ploughing operations — roving". 83 Squadron Hampdens were to attempt to strafe trains moving westwards towards France. One of the pilots at that briefing session was Guy Gibson, later to become famous as the leader of the Dam Busters. In his book, "Enemy Coast Ahead", he recalls those desperate days.

"Things were going badly in Belgium and France, but over in England fog came up regularly as if by the will of God to cover our fields and prevent us from operating."

Confirming the conditions of those days in May 1940 is Mr. Stan Harpham who was also present with Guy Gibson at that briefing on the 22nd May. Mr. Harpham, pilot of Hampden L4057, recalls: "That night the weather was hopeless — overcast and hazy."

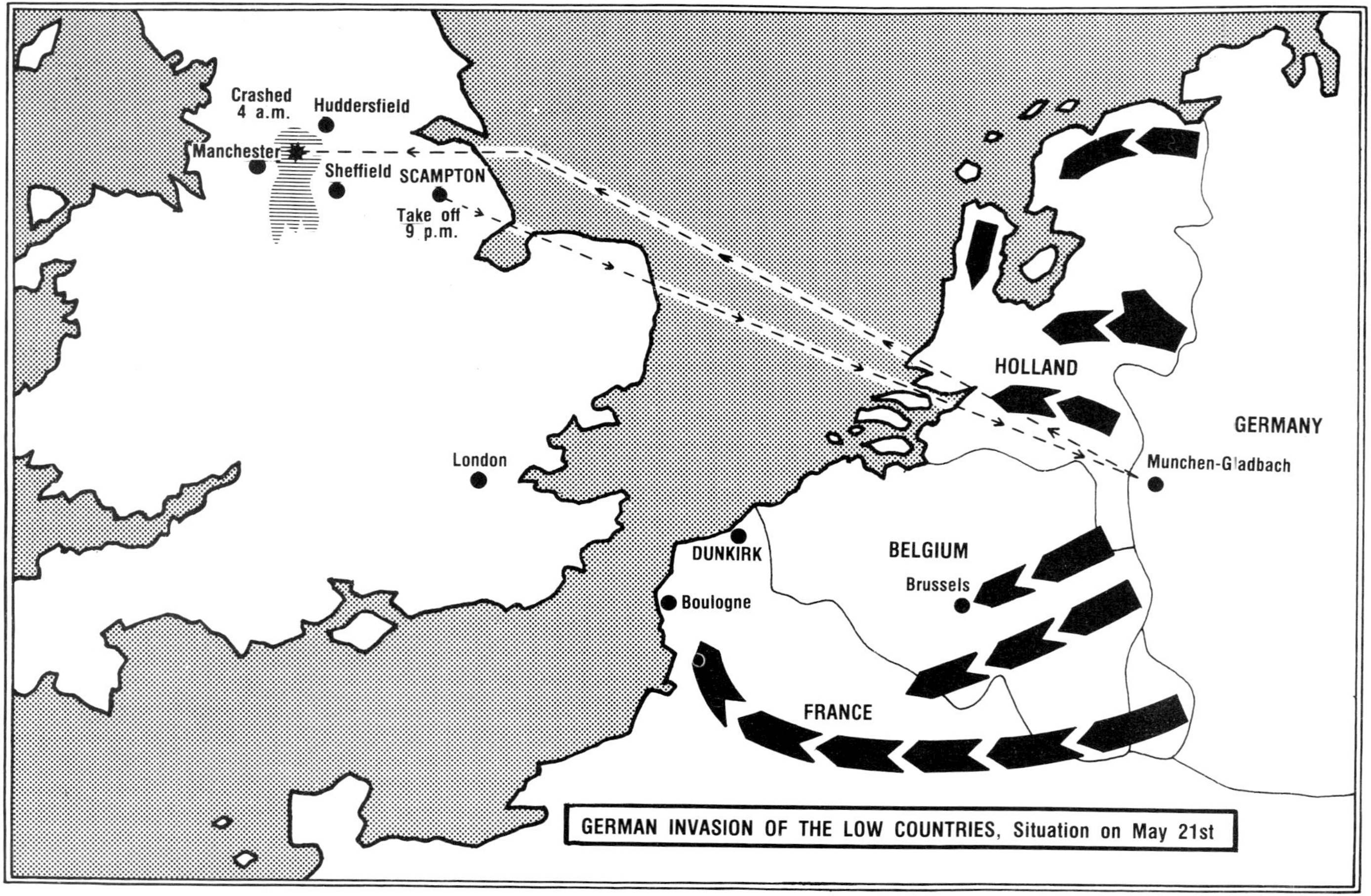

GERMAN INVASION OF THE LOW COUNTRIES, Situation on May 21st

Also at the briefing was a crew that had been brought together for the raid on Hitler's trains — the crew of Hampden L4055. It was to prove their first and last mission together.

In those early days of World War II there was a great deal of trial and error involved in bomber operations. Early raids on Germany bordered on the haphazard. Crews could choose their own routes to and from the target area; they could bomb from whichever height they chose; take-off time alone was decided for them.

In the words of another crewman present at the briefing, the then AC1 Ted Sayers, wireless operator/air gunner on L4058: "We were all beginners really — there was nothing to be done about it . . . one just got stuck in and learned about things as they happened — the hard way."

Against this background, the crew of the ill-fated L4055, could be considered experienced. Both pilot (Sergeant Jenkins) and lower gunner Sergeant Marsh, had flown seven previous missions. For A/C Thornton it was to be his first and last mission as wireless operator.

Sergeant Peter Josse was the Navigator — it was to be his third sortie. However, on those two previous occasions he had flown as air gunner. He was no novice when it came to navigation for he had twelve years' peace time service in the RAF, serving in Amman with 14 Squadron and in Egypt with 6 Squadron. By the standards of the day (spring 1940) he could be regarded as an experienced man.

It was dusk as the Hampden bombers of 83 Squadron moved from their dispersal points, each turning into the wind — then at five minute intervals, taking off and heading for Holland.

The crew in L4055 were the first away at 9.00. Guy Gibson in L4070 was the last up at 9.30. Seven bombers were heading for targets close to Germany's borders with Holland.

Radiating from the Munchen-Gladbach area was a railway system that was important to the German invasion. The Hampden crews were to seek out and bomb targets leading from this rail centre to the front.

Over Europe, the weather was against them yet despite this, five crews located targets and attacked with varying degrees of success. Squadron Leader Field caught two trains in a station at Gelden and destroyed both of them. Flight Lieutenant Collier and

Some 83 Squadron members May 1939 prior to the outbreak of hostilities. Sergeant Peter Josse is standing on the left. Behind them is Hampden 4048, the first aircraft of that type to be delivered to 83 Squadron.

his crew attacked a train near the German town of Emmerich but they were unable to observe any results. A remaining bomb was released over the aerodrome at Upenburg. Goods trains standing on a track near the town of Hasselt were caught by P/Officer Lyster and direct hits obtained and observed. Bursting flak peppered the aircraft and AC1 Sayers in the upper rear gun position lost the right heel of his flying boot — but there were no injuries.

P/Officer Bird and his crew made the longest trip that night when they flew to Neuss-Gruenbroich where they spotted two trains which they immediately tried to bomb. No results were seen and they climbed into the overcast and headed for Scampton.

Last up and last to leave the target area in a labouring L4070 was Guy Gibson. A railway bridge over the Schelde-Mass Canal was lined up in the bombsight by P/Officer Watson — cramped up in the nose. As they climbed away from the target area, it was observed to have sustained a direct hit. The most difficult target of all that night was destroyed — an indication of the flying skills of the pilot who was to become one of the best known flyers of the last war.

Navigator, Sergeant Peter Josse

Sergeant Harpham was unable to establish his position in the poor visibility as the weather worsened. After stooging around in the overcast for some time, he turned L4057 for home, retaining his bombs.

The crew of L4055 were also unable to identify a worthwhile target and Sgt. Jenkins set course out over the North Sea. They too were bringing their bombload home — bombs which would end up on a hillside at Holme, a small village near Holmfirth.

For the seven Hampdens approaching England, each making landfall at varying times after 2 a.m. a large weather front awaited them along the eastern coastline.

Mr. Harpham recalls the stress of that night as he sought to bring the craft and his crew safely down.

"We received a diversion to another field but our "Syko" code machine could only make out " . . .hall". I assumed from this that we were to locate Stradishall; however I was lucky enough to catch a glimpse of a beacon through the cloud and identified Mildenhall. After a desperate circuit or two the full aerodrome lights were put on and I somehow got in."

For Sgt. Jenkins in L4055 there was no chance sighting of an aerodrome beacon. He flew on, unaware of the diversion to the airfields of Norfolk where his fellow pilots were putting down.

Fifty miles from the coast they had been challenged over the radio by one of the MF/DF stations and had responded with the correct ID signal. But after that, nothing was

Pilot, Sergeant Stanley Jenkins

heard on the frequencies used to home in to the airfields.

During that last 50 miles the wireless must have given out — so without navigation aids — in bad weather — Sgt. Josse (who was navigating) would have been unable to assist Sgt. Jenkins to find an airfield.

After flying for some time above cloud with petrol getting low, Jenkins had two alternatives to consider; either risk dropping through cloud and attempting a landing where he could — or, bailing out. He opted for descent through cloud — in those days crews valued their charges highly and "she" had to be saved if at all possible.

An explosion awoke ARP warden Mrs. Doris Haigh at around 4 a.m. Hurriedly she dressed and made her way up to where she could see flames and smoke belching up from the corner of a hillside field at the side of Holme Moss.

Her attempts to reach the blazing wreck were thwarted as exploding ammunition sprayed the area around. She crouched behind a wall as 303 bullets struck the other side. It was almost light before she could get near — then she could see that her attempts to reach the aircraft had been in vain. The four crewmen had been killed on impact.

A week later, children playing near the wreckage found an unexploded bomb which was later exploded by Royal Engineers of the 35th Bomb Disposal Section. The wreckage of L4055 remained on the site throughout the summer and was finally removed in the winter of the same year. An eight man salvage team dismantled the remains and these were rolled down the hill to an awaiting Queen Mary trailer.

Today, at the crash site, there is a slight crater with a stream running through it and a partially-demolished wall which L4055 had tragically ploughed through.

The pilot, Sergeant Stanley Jenkins, and Navigator Peter Josse, were buried together with full military honours in the old churchyard at Nettleham, Lincolnshire.

Three days after the raid on the rail network, the British Army were lifted from the beaches of Dunkirk. Bomber Command's contribution to delaying the German advance could only have been minor. Bombloads were low, navigation aids were barely adequate, bombing techniques were, only just being developed — and crews were (by their own admission) novices for the most part.

With the wireless inoperative and in 10/10ths cloud, the crew of L4055 stood little chance — once in the vicinity of the fateful range of Pennine hills.

Crash site as it is today. Crater where a bomb was blown up can be seen in the foreground. The partially demolished wall remains as it was when L4055 flew through it. J. OWNSWORTH

No Mount For An Ace

Defiant N1766 of 96 Squadron, flying from Cranage to Digby and return, on night flying practise and air tests, abandoned when the engine failed, Crashed on Rowlee Pasture, April 12, 1941. Map reference 154905.

The sole passenger aboard the twin-engined Oxford was a black labrador by the name of "Skeeta". New Zealander Flight Lt. Walter Matthews was delivering him to the C.O. at 116 Squadron.

Skeeta's master, another New Zealand pilot by the name of Paul Rabone, had been posted missing on July 24th, 1944, whilst flying a daylight "ranger" mission over Germany in a Mosquito. Now the dog was being delivered to his new master.

Rabone had been in the process of building up a reputation as a fighter pilot at the time he went missing — his combat life to that date had been most eventful. He was among the few R.A.F. personnel who had arrived in France the day before war was declared on Germany in September 1939. By April 1941, he had baled out six times. The last time, he left his steed over Derbyshire — the wreckage of that machine lies around a crater on Rowlee Pasture above the Derwent Reservoir.

The first time Rabone was shot down was on a bombing raid on the German-held bridge at Maastricht.

Those early missions carried out by British bomber squadrons in vain attempts to slow down the mighty German Blitzkrieg were pitiful. Outdated and obsolescent Fairey Battles struggled through fields of flak thrown up by mobile anti-aircraft units — to drop their inadequate bomb loads around the bridge.

Rabone's Battle sustained severe flak damage and he with his other two crew members, was forced to bale out. They landed safely but found themselves behind German lines.

The roads in Belgium were thronged with refugees, fleeing they knew not where; Rabone and his crew disguised in civilian clothes, mingled with them and passed unnoticed by the advancing Germans.

Upon reaching Dieppe, Rabone found three Hurricanes — and using parts from two of them he managed to make the other flyable. Back in England, a short rest, then once again he was in France with his Squadron — only to be shot down for the second time.

On this occasion a Messerschmitt 109 caught him whilst he was on a bombing raid to destroy a bridge over the Seine. The Fairey Battle's defensive armament — a single forward-firing machine gun and a single machine gun manned by the wireless operator, were no deterrent to the attacking fighter and once more, Rabone and his crew abandoned their aircraft.

Paul Rabone and Skeeta

This time they found themselves at the right side of the front line and four days later they were back in England with 88 Squadron.

In August of 1940 he was posted to a fighter squadron and after some intensive training on Hurricanes at Drem in Scotland, Rabone was ready to give out some punishment to the enemy, as a change from being on the receiving end.

His opportunity came when in October the Squadron was posted to Tangmere, near the South coast. Although the Battle of Britain had been fought and won, there was still plenty of activity over the English Channel as Rabone discovered on his first patrol. Twenty thousand feet over Portsmouth he was attacked by 50 Me 109's — but managed to escape damage.

The following day Rabone was patrolling at 27,000 feet along with the fighters of five squadrons. The Wing met a formation of Me 109's and battle commenced. Rabone tagged on to a German fighter and shot it up. As he watched it spin away pouring black smoke, he felt the thump of bullets striking his Hurricane. Out of control — for the third time — the New Zealander jumped.

A safe landing at Dungeness, but a little too close to the sea for comfort.

Next day, Rabone bagged his second victim, another Me 109 — again he was raked with fire but struggled home. On landing he counted 32 bullet holes.

The month of November and another Me 109 fell to Rabone's guns — but now the young pilot was to move to another phase of his fighting career — night fighting.

Luftwaffe tactics underwent a change — the bombers came by night and the defences went over to the problems of night location and interception. It was during November that Rabone had to jump twice to save his life.

A severe storm at 22,000 feet caused him to make his first jump at night — he landed safely near Selsey Bill. Again at night, high over London on patrol, his engine stopped and refused to re-start — over the side again for the fifth time. A built up area — where would he land? The terrifying prospect of broken and smashed bones? Rabone floated neatly into London's Green Park!

During December, whilst with 96 Squadron, he was given a Night Visual Capacity Test — and the result was? Exceptional!

The Squadron moved up north for the night defence of the Liverpool area. It was at Cranage that Paul Rabone was introduced to the Bolton Paul Defiant — it was not to be a happy association and was to be climaxed by his sixth jump and the aircraft's remains left decorating a hill in the Peak District National Park, Derbyshire.

Introduced into Fighter Command in May 1940, the Defiant proved to be a failure. All the armaments of this two-seat fighter were concentrated in a single turret situated behind the pilot. It was impossible for the gunner manning four machine guns to anticipate his pilot's manoeuvres and to take aim. After heavy losses, against the more conventional forward-firing fighters, this type was switched to a night fighter role. 96 Squadron were among the recipients of this dubious steed.

Pilots of 96 did not take to the Defiant — its shortcomings were obvious to them and consequently they hung onto their Hurricanes and only very reluctantly took up the two-seater on patrol.

Paul Rabone was put in charge of A-flight which consisted of four aircraft, and placed on detachment at Squires Gate. He firmly marked the occasion by taking up a well-tried and proven 'Hurrybird' and shooting down his first enemy bomber at night — and those were the days before air to air radar — bringing his total of E/A destroyed to four.

Flying Officer Rabone had been ordered to patrol Formby at 14,000 feet; because of heavy cloud obscuring the ground he was out of position when he suddenly sighted the glow of exhausts — of a two-engined bomber slightly above him about fifty yards ahead.

Bringing the nose of his Hurricane up slightly he opened fire into the belly of the aircraft — which promptly dived.

Rabone followed and got in another burst which caused the bomber to catch fire as it dropped towards the sea off Blackpool.

In the months following, a number of mishaps with the newly-acquired Defiants did not endear that particular type to the pilots of 96 Squadron. There was a full moon and the weather was perfect for intercepting raiders on the 12th March, when more than the usual number of Defiants were airborne. Individual fighters were being vectored on to enemy raiders by ground control.

Rabone over Liverpool had to turn for base, Defiant N.1766 had suffered gun failure.

Another 96 Defiant crew actually spotted an enemy bomber and identified it as a Heinkel III. The pilot, Flight Sgt. Taylor lined the German bomber up for his gunner, but when Flight Sgt. Broughton attempted to fire, the guns jammed. The enemy bomber dived away steeply putting up defensive fire — as it happened no bullets made contact with the Defiant. Another Defiant which experienced similar problems did not get off so lightly.

Defiant N.1803 piloted by a Czechoslovakian, Flying Officer Vesley, intercepted another Heinkel III. His air gunner, Flight Sgt. Haycock filled his sights and operated the firing mechanism — nothing! The guns just failed to fire . . . Vesley formated on the bomber expecting his gunner to clear the trouble. Even when the German raider took evasive action Vesley followed him and determinedly flew alongside — all this time Haycock worked frantically on the four machine guns. Eventually, the starboard gunner on the bomber raked the persistent night fighter, and Vesley was hit in the head, chest, shoulder and left arm — and immediately lost consciousness.

When he came too, he found the Defiant in a spin — regaining control, the badly-injured pilot courageously brought his plane home and

1939/42 "DEFIANT"—The R.A.F.'s famous turret fighter, a single squadron of which destroyed, without loss, no fewer than thirty-seven enemy aircraft in one day at Dunkirk. The "Defiant" has also won an enviable reputation as a night fighter.

Photograph and caption reproduced from a booklet published in 1943 to commemorate 25 years of association between Boulton Paul and the RAF. Note the last sentence of the booklet's caption; perhaps not the sentiments shared by 96 Squadron pilots.

put it down safely.

The same night Flight Sgt. McNare intercepted another Heinkel and shot it down near Widnes — he was flying a Hurricane.

More frustration was to follow for the crews flying the Defiants. On the night of April 10th 1941 the expected Luftwaffe aerial attack on Birmingham materialised. The night fighter defences were ready — anticipating the enemy attack 96 Squadron joined up with 256 'Defiant' Squadron at Ternhill, which was 25 miles nearer the target city.

From the outset things began to go wrong for Defiant crews of 96. Out of the eight aircraft involved from that Squadron, only two managed to keep up a sustained patrol over the blitzed city — not one of the German raiders was sighted. The usual crop of failures and breakdowns dogged the Defiant crews causing the majority of machines to become unserviceable.

Rabone's Defiant N.3438 developed trouble 10,000 feet over the target city, when its hydraulic pump burst.

Truly a disappointing 'show' as far as the pilots were concerned — they seemed helpless to prevent the Luftwaffe from devastating the cities assigned to their protection. When they had operated with Hurricanes they had achieved some results, but since going over to their failure-prone Defiants everything had gone wrong. Morale was at a low ebb for 96 in the month of April 1941.

Two days later — on April 12th — Rabone baled out for the sixth and last time. Little flying was being done — certainly none by night — when Rabone took off in Defiant N.1766 — the same one that had let him and his airgunner Sergeant Irvine down the previous month when the guns had jammed over Liverpool. On this routine trip the crewman in the gun turret was — Flying Officer Ritchie. They were flying from Cranage to Digby in Lincolnshire and return, on night flying and airtests.

It was twenty-past nine on a black, cloudy night and they were twenty miles off track over the desolate Dark Peak area. At around 3,000 feet the two of them abandoned the machine which promptly thudded into Rowlee Pasture.

Both men landed safely, although Ritchie

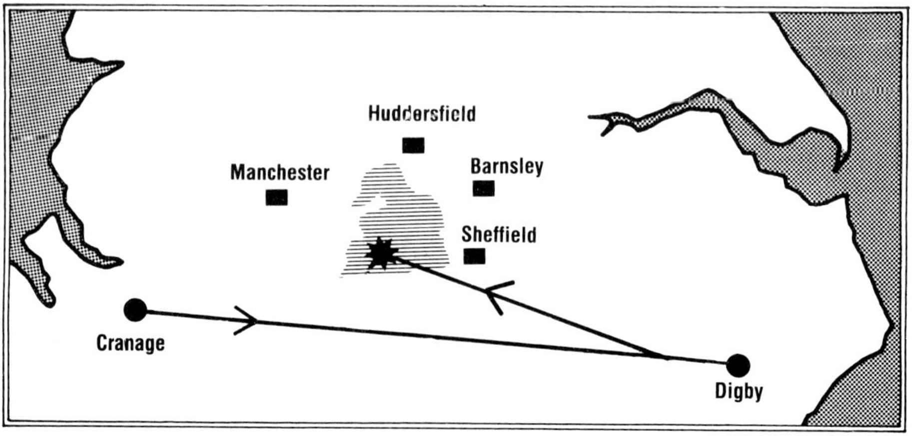

was cross-examined by a suspicious farmer who mistook him for a German flier. Through his Scottish accent Ritchie assured the puzzled local that he was truly British!

Over 40 years later, John Ritchie recalls the events of that night.

"We took off on a normal training flight and all went well on the outward journey.

"Coming back we were flying below cloud, but as the weather worsened Paul decided to climb above cloud, in view of the high ground we had to cross. At some point he called up and asked for a vector to base, to which he received a jumbled reply. Several more calls for assistance were put out but the replies were indecipherable. Shortly after this, the

John Ritchie

R/T packed up completely, and Paul informed me he was not very happy about the engine.

"We discussed the situation and having no R/T and not knowing where we were, we decided to abandon the aircraft, having gained a little more height.

"Having abandoned the aircraft and coming down, I saw water — and hoped I wouldn't land in that! Fortunately, the ground came up and hit me. I gathered up my parachute and set off down hill — but some way down decided the 'chute was a nuisance so I discarded it. I eventually came to a road and tossed a coin to see in which direction I should go. I didn't have too far to go, as I saw a faint light which I discovered was a farmhouse. I knocked at the door and was met by the farmer, brandishing his shot gun! The farmer was on the telephone and I asked him to inform the police, who arrived eventually and assured me that Paul has been picked up. One little courtesy was afforded by the police. They stopped at a pub, knocked up the landlord and got me a very large whisky — which I certainly needed!

"After de-briefing at the Squadron we were sent smartly back into the air again. . ."

Twenty days later Rabone was posted out to 85 Squadron as 'Supernumary for Flying' — a pilot extra to complement. At least this was a Squadron that used the Douglas Havocs as a nightfighter — and not the dreaded Defiant.

In June 1943 Rabone joined 23 Squadron in the Mediterranean theatre and teamed up with navigator Pilot Officer Johns — where they were engaged in intruder missions over Sicily and Italy flying Mosquitos. This duo shot up trains, bombed railways, destroyed vehicle convoys and on one occasion caught three seaplanes sitting on the water — wrecking them. The Mosquito was the perfect steed for them.

During this period Rabone brought down three more German bombers. As an intruder pilot he was rated "excellent".

In November 1943 he returned to England and seven months later the Allies invaded Europe; Rabone was posted to 515 Squadron, which until that time had only operated at night, and they were about to switch to daylight Ranger raids over Europe. An experienced day-ranger pilot was needed to show the other pilots the ropes.

On the 21st,June Rabone caught an ME 110 just taking off and shot it down in flames — the 515's first daylight victory. By the end of the month the pilots were claiming five German aircraft brought down — three of them were Rabone's, bringing his personal total of air victories to ten.

The following month he was posted back to 23 Squadron and on the 24th,July 1944 after 12 days leave, Paul Rabone and Flying Officer Johns took off on another day-ranger operation. From this mission they failed to return, and no trace has ever been found of them.

Rabone's dog, Skeeta, was passed to his new master and back in New Zealand his wife Pamela eventually re-married.

On a hillside in peaceful Derbyshire lies the shattered remains of the Defiant . . . an unworthy mount, but the only remaining memorial to the young New Zealand flier, Paul Rabone.

Scraps of metal gathered together into one pile. Numerous broken spades littering the crater give evidence of the activities of aviation archeology groups.
inset: The shattered supercharger.

Recovery

On a Sunday morning in August 1980 at 6 a.m. a group of ten men rendezvoused at the Snake Inn on the A57. They were about to undertake the recovery of a Merlin aero-engine, the power plant of Defiant N 1766.

The necessary procedure for a recovery had been gone through and permission had been granted.

It is no easy task to pull an aircraft engine out of the ground where it has lain for almost forty years, heavy winching gear is needed. On this occasion the required 'muscle' was to be provided by a powerful winch located on the front of a World War 2 vintage Dodge truck owned by Mr. Frank Derrick of Manchester. Another ex U.S. Army vehicle, a Willy's Jeep, completed the transport that would take the party to the wreck site high on Rowlee Pasture, above Derwent Valley.

As both vehicles had been restored to their former war-time livery complete with military markings, the small expedition appeared to have turned the clock back a full thirty-five years as it headed up the narrow farm tracks and out onto the open moor.

In the leading vehicle, Norman Winterbot-

Exposed — The engine that failed, laying firmly embedded in mud at the bottom of a deep hole.

tom acted as guide, as the party rolled across the soft peaty ground through the drifting morning mist.

The site was quickly located and the recovery team gathered around the water filled crater which measured approximately twenty feet across.

They took it in turns to bail out the water which was about four feet deep. After an hour of bailing the bucket struck metal. The top of the engine was uncovered and the winch hook attached. It took a couple of attempts to free the Merlin engine from the tight grip of the mud, then with a loud sucking noise it broke free.

Once free from the crater it was given a preliminary clean before being lifted into the back of the Dodge. With the extra weight, the return trip across Rowlee Pasture proved difficult as time and again the truck became bogged down. Not an easy journey but finally the engine arrived at a garage where it was given a thorough steam clean.

It is intended to put this example of the famous engine type on display.

The recovery of Defiant N 1766's Merlin

XX engine is typical of many such activities that have been going on in this country over the past ten or fifteen years. Numerous wreck recovery groups have come into being, enthusiasts who spend their spare time digging up, logging and researching aircraft crash sites.

Co-ordinating the efforts of these groups is the British Aviation Archaeological Council whose official publication 'Aviation Archaeologist', serves to inform subscribers of the activities of member groups in various parts of the country. This restricted publication is available through the post: Peter J. Moran, 154 Hardhorn Road, Poulton-Le-Fylde, Lancashire FY6 8ES.

The engine that failed, Paul Rabone's power plant receiving some attention from author Ron Collier. It is planned to put this historic engine type on exhibition.

Tail End Charlie

Wellington MK2 Rolls-Royce Merlin X Engines IWM

Wellington W5719 of 150 Squadron, returning to base at Snaith from a bombing raid on Cologne, crashed at Upper Tor, July 31, 1941. Map reference 111877.

In the early months of World War II both the Luftwaffe and RAF Bomber Command exercised restraint in the use of their bomber aircraft.

Each side wished to avoid reprisals by accidentally killing civilians in bombing raids; consequently, targets consisted mainly of the opposing nation's warships, plus harmless leaflet dropping excursions by the RAF at night over Germany.

With, however, the German invasion of the Low Countries in May 1940, the 'kid gloves' came off and concern for civilian life and property was abandoned. This took a particularly nasty turn for the worse as both the Luftwaffe and Bomber Command discovered that their attempts to destroy military targets, such as munitions factories, port installations and so on, were ineffective. The cities of the enemy were easier to locate, so both sides began a policy of deliberate attacks on civilian populations.

There followed a period of retaliation raids for example — the Luftwaffe bombed Coventry and Southampton so the RAF bombed Mannheim; Berlin was attacked which in turn provoked raids on London. Demoralising of the enemy nation by submitting the people to bombardment was the line of justification taken by the leaders. But rather than destroying the people's will to fight on, the bombing of civilians served instead to strengthen their resolve to "see it through together".

As a policy of strategy it was ineffective but was to be continued until the war ended.

For the RAF bomber crews who had to carry out the orders of the policy-makers, the locating of a German city at night and the releasing of explosives on it often proved a difficult task in those early days before effective navigational aids.

Daylight excursions over enemy territory by bombers had been abandoned for the most part by Bomber Command — it had proved too costly in men and machines. Consequently, two-engined Hampdens, Whitleys and Wellingtons with insignificant bomb loads took off at night — frequently in unfavourable weather conditions, for a German city perhaps situated on the Rhine — some 400 miles distant.

The round trip could take up to six hours with the crews in uncomfortable, cramped, cold and draughty conditions — fired at by anti-aircraft defences and night-fighters.

It was during this period of pioneer bombing of German cities that a Wellington, returning with its bomb load, hit a hillside in Edale, exploded — flinging clear the rear gun turret and its occupant.

It was July 1941; 150 Squadron moved that month from Newton in Nottinghamshire to Snaith in Yorkshire. It had been a bad period for 150 Squadron — they had suffered heavy losses during the month — at one time only two aircraft remained from a full complement of 12 aircraft and 2 reserve.

Among the replacements for 150 Squadron at Snaith was Sergeant Tilley who was to

Squadron photograph showing the pilot Sgt. Parrott, next to him is the wireless operator Sgt. Webber. On a line with them at the end is Sgt. Monk.

experience an amazing escape on the last day of July.

Earl Tilley joined the crew of 'S' for sugar as rear gunner — in most cases the most dangerous crew position in a bomber. German night fighters would invariably attack that position first; if 'Tail-End Charlie' was hit, usually the fate of the bomber was sealed.

Through the official pipeline came the order for another night sortie for 150 Squadron. Executive Orders for Operation No. 6, the bombing of Cologne, using eight aircraft on the night of July 30th, 1941.

Weather conditions throughout the day were bad — low cloud covered the base and heavy rain drenched the runways. It looked, to the waiting crews, as if the operation might be cancelled; and they would spend that night in their beds rather than 15,000 feet over the North Sea and Germany.

The eight Wellingtons had each been loaded with a one 1000 lb. bomb and four or five 500 pounders — and now stood in the pouring rain, awaiting the crews.

At 10.30 in the evening, the rain abated and the crews began to move out to their machines. Even during the checks that the crews had to carry out the raid could have been cancelled, but the rain held off and at 11.20 p.m. the first bomber was in position for take-off.

'S' for sugar was to be the first one off the ground piloted by Sergeant Parrott; second pilot was Sergeant Haswell. Navigating the 450 miles to Cologne and back was Canadian, Sergeant Evelle. Wireless Operator was Sergeant Webber.

Protecting Wellington W5719, 'S' for sugar, crouched up in the nose turret was Sergeant Denis Monk from Stockport. Taking care of possible stern attacks was Canadian, Sergeant Earl Tilley — 'Tail-End Charlie'.

There was to be no cancellation and at 11.25 p.m. 'S' for sugar was climbing into the overcast sky followed twenty minutes later by a second Wellington — with the rest following at five minute intervals. By ten past one the Squadron had been swallowed up and forty-eight men were en route for Germany — five of them were not to return to Snaith — and one would not return for six months.

From his isolated position at the tail, Earl Tilley observed the events of that tragic flight.

"We ran into heavy cloud over the North Sea — and after we crossed the enemy coast we flew into a bad electrical storm with thunder and lightning all around us.

"We tried to climb over the storm and then to go round it, with no success. Our Skipper decided to return to base with our bomb load.

Earl Tilley

When we reached the English coast the cloud cover had moved in. To make matters worse, our radio had been rendered u/s by the electrical storm.

"Our navigator figured that we had crossed the coast in the vicinity of the Wash. All of us were looking for an opening in the cloud trying to see something that we could identify to establish our position.

"Our Skipper must have dropped through the clouds when he estimated that we should have been over our base."

"The next thing I remember, I was lying on the ground and the aircraft was burning. I tried to get away from the crash as I realised that we still had that bomb-load. I remember having great difficulty in trying to walk — I crawled and rolled away — then lost consciousness.

"The next thing I recall was hearing voices and it was daylight. I was taken to a house in a nearby village and from there to a hospital in Manchester."

Six months later Earl Tilley returned to 150 Squadron at Snaith, only to be shot down again over Holland in June 1942 and taken prisoner.

Wellington W5719 had struck Edale Moor at Upper Tor. The impact and resulting explosion had blown clear the rear turret and its occupant, Sergeant Tilley.

Of the other seven aircraft which had set out to bomb the citizens of Cologne, five found their target and bombed a large fire that they found burning there. The heavy cloud stretched over the city and they were unable to see any results from their bombing. Two other Wellingtons bombed alternative targets in Belgium.

Manning the rear gun turret of a British bomber over Germany may have proved to be the most dangerous crew position — but should a flying accident occur, there were definite advantages in being 'Tail - End Charlie'.

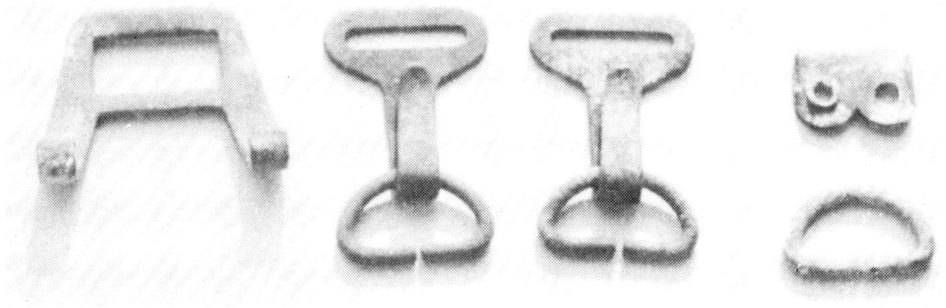

Buckles and harness clips found at the crash site. OWNSWORTH COLLECTION

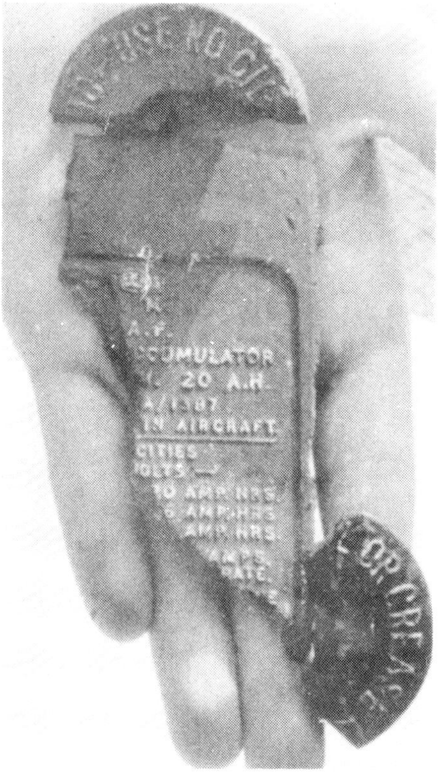

Fragments of bakelite

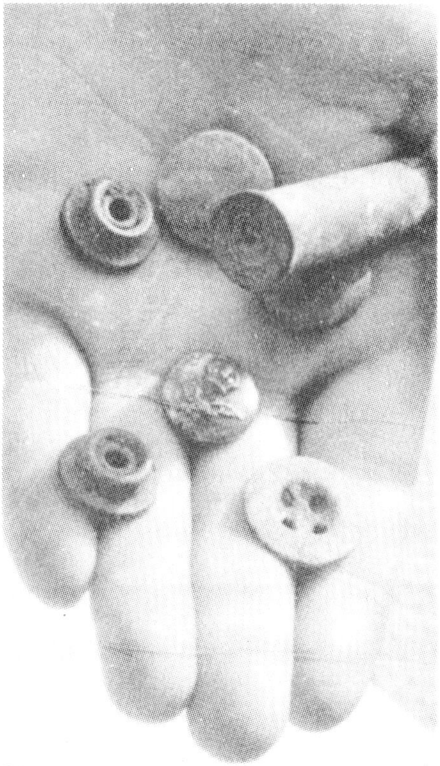

Uniform buttons and cartridge case

The only visible remains on the hillside at the crash site.

Westland Lysander SA, 900 h.p. Mercury XX Engine IWM

South West By North East

Lysander V9403 of 6 Anti-aircraft Co-operation Unit flying from Ringway to Rhyl for training duties, turned on a wrong heading and crashed on Slate Pit Moss, August 19, 1941. Map reference 041033.

In the early hours of 19th August, 1941, a Lysander of 6 Anti-Aircraft Co-operation Unit crashed on the moors above Chew Valley, trapping the pilot and wireless operator in the wreckage. For two days the injured men lay awaiting rescue and the pilot watched helplessly as an air search went on just three miles away — centred around an aircraft wreck from the previous year. The following is Pilot Officer Hoddinott's, own account of the accident.

My story begins on the 18th August, 1941 at which time I was a pilot officer in the Royal Air Force. The Unit in which I was serving at that time was an Anti-Aircraft Co-operation Unit, stationed at Ringway Airport, Manchester; one of the duties of which was to provide aircraft by day and night for the training of Anti-Aircraft Guns and Searchlight Units.

I think it is true to say that I was one of the more experienced members of the Unit having completed more than one thousand hours flying as pilot on some sixteen different types of single and twin-engined aircraft.

On the night of 18th/19th August I was detailed to fly a Lysander Aircraft to the Rhyl area for two hours co-operation with Guns and Searchlights there.

In these comparatively early days of the war, being classed as a non-operational unit, our aircraft, although armed, were not equipped with Radio Telephony and the only navigational aid which we could obtain was by Wireless Telegraphy through the medium of a W/T operator. These night sorties could therefore only be carried out in reasonable weather conditions.

I arrived at the airfield in ample time for a 2.30 a.m. take-off and studied the weather forecast for the area provided by the Meteorological Office. This reported five tenths cloud at 2,000 feet, in other words half the sky would be covered in cloud with the cloud base at a height of 2,000 feet above sea level. Not a particularly good forecast for the job which I had to do but worth trying so I advised my wireless operator and the duty pilot in the control tower that I would be taking off as planned.

Together with my wireless operator I proceeded to the aircraft, started up the engine, carried out the usual pre-flight cockpit and engine tests and taxied out to the take-off position. Here again I carried out the usual checks and also set my gyro-compass by reference to the magnetic compass.

For the benefit of the lay-reader I should explain that the gyro-compass is basically a calibrated card mounted on a gyroscope, and uses the gyroscopic principle of rigidity. It is therefore a much more stable directional reference than the magnetic compass which is north seeking and is affected by acceleration, deceleration and turning. Due to the rotation of the earth however precession takes place and it is necessary to re-set the gyro indicator by reference to the magnetic compass, at frequent intervals during flight.

I then proceeded to take-off into wind along the line of five small battery operated glim lamps, invisible from the air above a height of about one thousand feet.

At five hundred feet and still climbing I turned to circle the airfield and set course for Chester so as to avoid the balloon barrage at Liverpool. We flew into the cloud at less than two thousand feet but this did not worry me in view of the met. forecast of only five tenths cloud.

Over the intercom I could hear my wireless operator trying to contact the ground station to obtain the usual bearing to confirm that we were following the correct course, and everything appeared to be just another routine flight.

We had been flying for about fifteen minutes with no sign of a break in the cloud and I decided that it was time to check the directional gyro indicator with the magnetic compass and was surprised to find that there was a difference of about 160° between the two instruments, and instead of flying on

Pilot Officer Hoddinott

south westerly course I was in fact on a north north easterly heading.

I decided that the directional gyro was faulty and instead of flying on a straight course I had been following the directional gyro in a very gradual turn to starboard. If my deductions were correct I could be dangerously close to the balloon barrage over Liverpool and I was still flying in cloud at 2,500 feet — not a very healthy position to be in. I therefore immediately turned on to a southerly course on the magnetic compass and decided to reduce height in order to break clear of the cloud. My estimation of our position at that time was that we were to the north of Chester a low lying area where I could quite safely reduce height to 1,000 feet.

Even in the blackout and on the darkest of nights one could always pick out the railway marshalling yards at Chester and also the outline of the Dee estuary. I reduced speed and commenced a gradual descent.

At 2,000 feet we were still in cloud — then with the altimeter registering just over 1,900 feet the dark grey of the cloud suddenly changed to pitch black — we had struck the ground

I must have been knocked unconscious as the next recollection I have was that I was in a half sitting, half reclining position on the remains of the wrecked aircraft. The windscreen instrument panel, the cockpit and the engine cowlings had all disappeared and what remained of the engine was a mess of twisted metal forced back against my legs and there was a strong smell of burning oil.

My thoughts immediately went to the petrol tank situated just behind me which must still have been three parts full and wondered if the whole lot would go up in flames. I was unable to turn round but asked my wireless operator if he was all right. His reply cut me to the quick, it was "I thought you were supposed to be a good pilot!" I was later to learn that his parting words to his wife the evening before were that she had nothing to worry about because he was flying with me that night. He too, although not badly injured was trapped by the legs.

I tried to release my legs but only succeeded in pulling my left leg out of my flying boot leaving that firmly wedged in the wreckage of the engine. Once the danger of fire had passed I was not unduly worried as I was sure that with the arrival of daylight we should very soon be found. I was not in any pain, no doubt due to shock and the severity of my injuries.

I remember seeing what appeared to be a large lake a short distance ahead but with the arrival of daylight this turned out to be a piece of engine cowling just a few feet ahead of the wreckage.

Another surprise also awaited with the arrival of dawn. I had expected to see fields and trees and hedges and possibly a farmhouse but instead there was nothing but barren moorland as far as the eye could see.

From time to time I leaned forward to try to move some of the engine wreckage and release my right leg but I must have been very weak, when I leaned forward blood dripped freely from my forehead and I was obliged to lay back again without having made any progress.

As the day wore on my Wireless Operator became very despondent frequently praying and telling me that no-one would ever find us. I could not see him as he was trapped in the rear half of the fuselage but gathered from what he said that he could not see outside. It must have been harder for him, at least I was out in the open air, and would be able to see if there was any sign of activity in the surrounding countryside. I was to be disappointed however. I had no idea of the time because my watch had been torn off my wrist in the crash, but I estimated that it must have been late afternoon when I saw an aircraft circling in the distance. I recognised it as one of the several types with which my unit was equipped and was confident that the pilot was searching for us.

The aircraft continued circling over an area some considerable distance from us and although I still had the Very cartridges in the pocket of my flying suit I could not use them because the Very pistol was buried somewhere in the wreckage, as also was the torch which I invariably took with me at night. I told my Wireless Operator that the aircraft was obviously searching for us and I felt sure that it would not be long now before we were found but once again we were to be disappointed because it eventually made off in the opposite direction without having seen us, and it was our fate to spend yet another night among the wreckage.

I learned later that the aircraft was in fact one from my unit searching for us and that the pilot had spotted the wreckage of an aircraft and had directed a search party to it only to find that it was an old wreckage which had been there for several months. It was then too late to continue the search that day.

During the night we heard air-raid sirens sounding which raised our hopes of rescue because we felt that the Home Guard and Wardens would be out and about but what we did not seem to appreciate at the time was that we were in a virtually uninhabited area.

With the arrival of dawn my greatest concern seemed to be my terrific thirst. It rained a little and although I turned my face to the sky not a drop found its way into my mouth.

The day wore on without further incident and as daylight was beginning to fade again a man appeared stumbling towards us as rapidly as the rough ground would permit.

I told my Wireless Operator that a man was coming whereupon he shouted at the top of his voice urging the man to hurry and continued to do until our rescuer was actually standing beside the wreckage.

I was desperately thirsty and asked the man to remove the batteries from my torch case and fill it with water from the ditch. He said that I couldn't drink that because it was peat water but I must have been very insistent because he did as I requested and I am sure that was the most refreshing drink I ever had.

Here I should say that although I had thought that night was approaching and the light was fading it was only mid-day, I was probably drifting towards death's door.

My recollection of events from here on are not quite so distinct. I remember the man leaving and returning some time later with several others. Two of them pulled away the wreckage of the engine with what appeared to be the greatest of ease and I was lifted from the wreckage and laid on a stretcher. I was then carried for a considerable distance over rough ground and through at least one stream. I remember feeling the water on my back when one of the stretcher bearers must have lost his footing. I also remember arriving at the waiting ambulance being given a drink of hot sweet tea from a saucer. I would very much have liked more but the ambulance men were anxious to get moving.

The next thing I remember is lying in the hospital bed under a framework of electric lamps. The first few days in the hospital at Ashton-under-Lyne must have been a series of periods of consciousness and unconsciousness, but due to the untiring efforts of the surgeons and the constant devotion of the nursing staff I was soon well on the road to recovery.

The history of my recovery however is another story, let it suffice to say that after sixteen weeks I was well enough to be moved to a Royal Air Force hospital and after a further nine weeks was fit enough to return to my Unit for three months non-flying duties. I was then passed fit for flying duties and completed a further nine hundred hours flying as pilot and captain of aircraft before the war ended.

My Wireless Operator was not so fortunate, he died a few days after our admission to hospital, although I was not allowed to discover this fact until some two months later. I understand that he did not suffer such serious injuries as I did and that this was probably a contributory factor to his death.

As the surgeon who cared for me, wrote in a letter to me after my recovery, "There has been a good deal of discussion lately in the Medical Press with regard to deaths resulting from "crush injuries" — the point being that when a limb is compressed and its blood supply is interfered with the limb swells up but on the removal of the obstruction, the kidneys get damaged and death results from this cause. In your case your wounds were left open for many days and I am inclined to think that the "poisons" accumulated in your limb worked out of the open wounds and so your kidneys and your life were saved!"

It was not until I was well on the way to recovery that I was able to reason out exactly what had happened leading up to the crash. Until this time I had been convinced that the altimeter had been faulty, but then I asked my wife to bring me a map so that I could see where the hospital was and so the approximate position of the crash. It was only then that I realised that there was nothing wrong with the altimeter, we had in fact crashed on the top of the Pennines where they reach a height of almost two thousand feet above sea level.

It was in fact the directional gyro which was faulty and instead of flying in a west south westerly direction I had flown on a north easterly course.

Unlike Corrigan who achieved fame by taking off from an airfield on the east coast of America saying that he was flying to the west and landed in Ireland having flown across the Atlantic, I achieved — almost — oblivion.

On the 40th anniversary of his crash Mr. Hoddinott returned to the site where only a few shattered pieces of wood remain to mark the spot.

Wellington MK 1A

KLIMCZAK

Master Bomber

Wellington DV810, of 21 Operational Training Unit, flying on a night exercise from Edge Hill — got lost in bad weather and crashed on Broomhead Moor, December 9, 1942. Private land.

It was the foulest weather he had yet experienced while airborne. Nothing in his previous tour of operations with 214 Squadron of bombing sorties to Europe had prepared him for this.

"Tubby" Baker was annoyed at the situation he had been forced into by the 'powers that be'.

Right up to take off he had questioned the advisability of going. His insistence had caused the Officer Commanding Flying at Edge Hill, to check with his superiors at Wing HQ — but to no avail; the instructions were to go. So there he was, around 4,000 feet up approaching the east coast on a night cross country flight in Wellington DV810 in the midst of thick cloud and buffeted by high winds — with a trainee crew.

From the time they had climbed into the black overcast at Edge Hill, which was a satellite of 21 Operational Training Unit at Moreton-in-the-Marsh, they were on 'dead reckoning'. Already they had discovered that the forecast winds amounted to little more than a fairy story. The reality was now pushing them about all over the night sky — yes, Flying Officer Baker was definitely annoyed!

Of course, new aircrews were needed all the time and the demands placed on OTU's to turn them out were pressing. The OC's Flying were being pushed to produce crews, not only to replace those lost over Germany and for the formation of brand new squadrons, but also crews for Coastal Command, the Middle East and the Far East. OTU training came at the end of a long period of flying training for each individual. When individuals reached Bomber Command they were then formed into crews and given what amounted to a specialist course in bomber operations. It was a five months course involving 80 hours' flying time.

The education of a crew member cost a staggering £10,000. Actual training was undertaken by instructors who themselves were front line crew members and were 'resting' between operations.

There was a continual shortage of men with operational experience who could serve as instructors, especially pilots. Consequently, those who were suitable instructors had to work overtime during their 'rest' periods between operations. The risks were many as they were expected to undertake dangerous flying conditions to process men through the system.

Conditions experienced by the trainee crews, however, and the instructors of the six Wellingtons that took off on the night of December 9th, 1942 were far beyond what was reasonable.

That was Tubby Baker's considered opinion as the poor trainee navigator suggested that they must have reached their turning point, and gave a course change to take them back home to base. He accepted the navigator's judgment — after all, with all that muck swirling around them and high winds flinging them about like a cork in the ocean, the lad's guess as to their position seemed as good as anyone else's.

The pilot under training was Sergeant Turner. He dutifully turned onto the new heading. It was not a dual control aircraft and Baker could only oversee the pupil's actions and make suggestions.

"We have got gas bags on the RT Skipper!" came the urgent call from Sergeant Morgan, who was the Screen Wireless Operator (Instructor).

Balloons defending industrial cities had a small transmitter attached which emitted a warning signal so that Allied aircraft could avoid them. Wellington DV810 was flying blindly towards anti-aircraft balloons, the cables of which could disintegrate a propellor or take off a wing. Turner was gripping the control column and staring out into the blackness in front, his nervousness apparent.

"I'd better take over — out you come," Baker motioned the pupil to leave the controls.

Wing Commander "Tubby" Baker

Exchanging places in those circumstances was a risky business. Once at the controls, Baker checked their heading. Westerly! The sound of the balloon squeakers was in no way diminishing so he turned north to avoid being plucked from the sky — but the squeaks persisted. Taking the opposite direction they encountered the squeakers again — and it soon became clear that they were stooging around over a large industrial area.

They had to get down below cloud and establish their position — for they could not stay up there for ever, and there was no sign of the weather clearing. Coming down in their present position was out of the question. Balloons, factory chimneys, possible high ground — all ruled out that possibility. Baker announced his decision to the crew. He would head to the east, once out over the North Sea he would safely drop beneath the clouds, head due west picking up the coast, where their position could be established accurately.

Every one of the seven men on board — the two instructors and five trainees — knew that they were in a dangerous situation. They were hopelessly lost.

After twenty minutes of flying in an easterly direction, Baker decided that they must be well out over the North Sea and he proceeded to descend through the cloud.

"We came out at 1,200 feet — but saw what looked like another layer of cloud below us. I switched on my landing lamp which in the Wellington was housed in the wing, and shone straight down until operated by a lever from the cockpit. Although this layer seemed a strange colour, it did look like cloud and I switched off the landing light."

"Almost immediately there was a bang and my port engine was on fire. I realised that what I had thought to be cloud below us was the ground — and I shouted to the crew to brace themselves for a crash. I throttled back both engines and began to hold off. Reaching up I opened my escape hatch and from the light of the blazing port engine, belly landed. I ordered the crew out and scrambled clear myself."

DV810 erupted into a mass of flames and game birds evacuated the area in panic. Light from the burning aircraft lit up the surrounding countryside and revealed large clumps of heather. They were on wild moorland, but where precisely?

Baker assembled the crew and apart from being shaken, they were unharmed. He ordered them away from the wreck as he expected it to explode; he was right for when they got away to a safe distance, the aircraft blew up.

They decided not to continue to wander around, lost, but to stay where they were until daylight. There was the danger of walking over a cliff edge, considering their position near to the coast.

Baker was still annoyed. They could easily have all been killed. Had this been a bombing raid, the operation would have been called off because of the weather conditions — so why should a training flight be any different?

After about an hour of sitting in the heather watching the aircraft wreckage being consumed by fire, they saw lights and heard voices approaching. Help was coming at last, probably the inhabitants of a coastal village.

The crew was led off the moor and taken to Stocksbridge — which is approximately 70 miles from the east coast. They had indeed been well and truly lost.

While the crew was taken to hospital suffering from mild shock, Baker was given a bed at the local police sergeant's house. "I was treated very kindly indeed, by the sergeant's wife," he recalls. "And I was sorry that so much of my blood — from a gash on my head received during my hasty exit from the aircraft — was left on her pillows. For a long time after the event, the lady sent cakes to my Unit, for which I was most grateful."

Once back at Edge Hill, Baker received an order to report to the Officer Commanding Flying Wing at Moreton. The OC was in a black mood as F/O Baker entered his office and saluted.

"Baker! What do you mean by crashing one of my bloody aircraft?" thundered the OC, furious.

Baker was not a man to suffer fools gladly. Fixing the OC with a blazing eye he retorted, "What do YOU mean by sending me off in such bloody awful weather?"

As far as Baker was concerned, there was nothing more to be said. The OC, eager to amass flying hours, had made a wrong judgment. He spun on his heels and stormed out of the office. They could take whatever action they liked against him — but to risk the lives of men so unnecessarily was, to him, a far greater crime than his insubordination.

It is significant that nothing was said about the incident in the OC's office that day.

Of the other five Wellingtons that had taken off that stormy night, not one managed to return to Edge Hill. One of the five crashed at Manston. Baker's skill in putting Wellington DV810 down onto Broomhead Moor, with only the light from a blazing port engine to guide him, without harm to his crew, was indicative of what was to come. As was his handling of his superior officer.

By the time the war had ended, Tubby Baker had reached the rank of Wing Commander and was commanding his own squadron. He had collected four decorations; the citation for his last, the Bar to the Distinguished Service Order, read as follows:

"Wing Commander Baker has completed one hundred sorties, all of them against strongly-defended enemy targets. He has displayed the highest qualities of skill and

An Operational Training Unit preparing for night exercises IWM

bravery and throughout his devotion to duty has been unfailing. Undeterred by the heaviest opposition, Wing Commander Baker has invariably pressed home his attacks with the greatest resolution. His achievements have won high praise."

An example of the type of operation that prompted the words "pressing on against all odds" is seen in a sortie carried out on March 27th, 1943. Flying Officer Baker as he then was, learning of the formation of an elite Bomber Group that would lead and mark targets for the Main Bomber Force, he volunteered.

In March, 1943 he joined the newly-formed Pathfinder Force with his posting to 7 Squadron operating Stirling bombers at Oakington. As the month ended, Baker's flying skills were put to the test.

Target for the night of the 27th was "Big B" — Berlin. In the event, the raid itself was not a success. For various reasons, there were six early returns in 7 Squadron, and consequently there was a shortage of markers dropped on the target.

Baker, in Stirling R9255, reached the target and came in straight and level as a supporter to bomb the indicators dropped by his fellow Pathfinders. They were coned by searchlights and began to sustain hits by flak. The port outer engine was peppered by shrapnel and stopped. Loss of power in the port inner compounded the problem as Baker took evasive action to duck out of the blinding lights.

Having lost a great deal of height, and with reduced engine power making it impossible to regain it, Baker asked his navigator for a new route home; a route which would avoid high ground and known defences. With two healthy engines roaring away on the starboard wing and not much doing in the way of power on the port side, the Stirling was difficult to control on that long homeward trip.

After five exhausting hours (making a total of eight and a quarter) nursing the struggling bomber, Oakington was reached. Their trials were not quite over however.

Baker selected "undercarriage down" and three green lights lit up indicating that all units were locked down. They were all set for landing — what they could not know was that the port tyre had been sliced through by shrapnel!

At the instance of touchdown, the stricken monster slewed hard to port shearing away the high, ungainly undercarriage. The aircraft came to rest close to a cottage on the perimeter of the airfield and six weary men climbed out, shaken but unhurt.

Baker's skill and determination as a bomber pilot began to be recognised and in July, 1944 he was given command of 635 Squadron. After D Day he acted as Master Bomber on seventeen occasions.

On July 18th, 1944 the Second Army under General Montgomery , prepared to advance south of Caen. For three hours after dawn the heaviest concentrated air attack to date in support of ground forces took place. One of the targets was the village of Cagny which housed concentrations of German infantry and anti-tank guns. The village was the target for the Pathfinder Force.

Master Bomber for Cagny was Tubby Baker. One hundred bombers were directed onto the target by the newly-promoted Wing Commander. After the attack a gigantic smoke pall was suspended over the target like a shroud. The village of Cagny had been accurately obliterated.

When nations engage in acts of mass destruction against one another, inevitably men with certain qualities appear. The necessity of the times cause them to emerge from the masses of fighting men to take on positions of leadership and responsibility. Master Bomber, Wing Commander Stanley (Tubby) Baker DSO and Bar, DFC and Bar, was such a man. Glimmers of his qualities as a pilot and leader could be seen in the happenings that took place on the night of December 9th, 1942, when he crashlanded a Wellington on Broomhead Moor, saving his own life and those of his trainee crew.

A sheet of armour plate and an oxygen bottle are all that remain on Broomhead Moor.

Bouncing Bomber

Wellington III 1WM

Wellington X3348 of 427 Squadron, returning to base at Croft from a bombing raid on Lorient, crashed Blackden Edge, January 26, 1943. Map reference 129877.

Towards the end of January 1943 the British Admiralty instigated the order to bomb two targets in occupied France. There was the likelihood of heavy loss of life among French civilians, but it was considered a regrettable but necessary expedient of war.

German U-boats, operating from French ports in the Bay of Biscay, were causing heavy losses among Allied convoys in the Atlantic — they had to be stopped, even if this meant the sacrifice of civilians lives.

The Atlantic ports of St. Nazaire and Lorient were the targets for the night of the 25th.

There was little hope of doing any real damage to the U-boats for they lay in their lairs protected from air attack by many feet of reinforced concrete. At that date the RAF Bomber Command did not possess a bomb that would penetrate the U-boat pens. Most that could be hoped for was the destruction of outside machinery shops and service facilities that were in the surrounding dockyard area.

For the crews of 427 (Lion) Squadron RCAF those January days had presented them with frustrating cancellations and days of no flying because of weather conditions. Out of four minelaying sorties detailed for the Squadron in the days prior to the Lorient raid, three were cancelled at the last minute. A nerve/racking experience for the crews who were tensed up in their Wellingtons awaiting the order to go.

Nine aircraft from 427 Squadron No. 6 Group were detailed for the raid and stood bombed up on the runway at Croft, Co. Durham, on the afternoon of the 25th.

For the crew of Z for Zebra it was their fourth mission — they considered themselves veterans and keenly felt their battle experience in the presence of two newcomers to their crew.

The six of them would undergo a new experience as that day ended; they would descend a hill that they had never gone up. Partly responsible for the experience was the Navigator of X3348, Z for Zebra, Pilot Officer Martin. His story now follows:

Pilot Officer Martin

"As one of the few men who enjoy the distinction of having walked down a mountain without first walking up it, I feel entitled to tell my story, saying how it was done.

"In those days I was being paid to navigate an aircraft of the Royal Canadian Airforce, with an American-Swede as pilot, a Batley Yorkshireman as bombardier, a Welshman as wireless-operator-airgunner, and a boy from Durham as reargunner. I am a Londoner.

"On this occasion, we, being veterans of three operational flights, had a new pilot along, to show him how things were done. It was to be an eye-opener for him!

"On the 26th January, 1943 we assembled at Wellington Zebra; we had a different w/op/ag, as Taffy Baker, our regular man, had a cold, and I am sure he and the new pilot were suitably awed by our knowledgeable chatter about courses, heights, airspeed, weather and so on. I feel I should explain that we were veterans only on a survival basis. Our experience was limited, but we were alive to pass on even our small store.

"We were going to a quiet little spot called Lorient on this occasion, and barring errors of navigation, (my department) which might put us over an unexpected defended area, we anticipated no bother.

"Other people, whom we knew, had been to Lorient and had not come back, but that sort of thing was not for us. How cocky could you get on the strength of three trips?

"At ten minutes to five, on this January afternoon, our two motors poured life into Wellington Zebra, and whatever we had omitted to do must now wait five hours or so, for we were airborne. Carl Taylor, our "driver-airframe", (who had the thoroughly-approved ambition to return to Pensecola, in the U.S. of A. to meet the U.S.A.F. pilot who checked him out of the U.S.A.F. as unsuitable for flying heavy aircraft), set our first course on his compass. I settled down to try to see that he flew that course. This was a conflict of skills which finally generated quite astonishingly flying!

"From the point of view of operational flying, the journey went without incident.

"The bombardier, Don Mortimer, was the busiest bloke, spotting landmarks to assist my navigation, pumping oil on the well-known Zwicky and pump at the necessary intervals, checking his bombsight, his front turret and guns, and standing by for that moment that always made my heart miss a couple of beats, that moment when we changed off from overload to main petrol tanks. We had a very good idea when this detail was due, and Don would stand by the change-over cocks. We always flew till the motors checked in their steady beat, then over to main tanks, the motors roared on, and even a not very keen ear could hear us all start breathing again. We were a pretty average crew, so I expect this reaction was general.

"Lorient came, bombs went down, flak came up, Lorient went. Some days before we had done the same trip, and a very keen and accurate battery at Lannion, near the French coast, had nearly "got the coconut".

"This time we were very alert and on course, and speed, and time-at-turning-point out of the target. I like to think it was all very efficient and impressive to our pupil pilot.

"Now we settled to the routine of going

home, and I, as a keen navigator, decided to improve the hour with a bit of astro-navigation, taking sextant shots of stars, (definitely all the rage then). I passed the course to fly to the pilots, time at our turning point for course alteration for base, and a couple of light-beacon pin points near our route with which they could check our progress.

"Well, there I was, the very model of a good navigator, practising to improve his skill, when the drivers reported a cloud ahead, and their intention to let down to fly below it. So I returned to my "office" to check our position, and prepare to use any landmark which might be seen and to work on my 1st 'star fix'. The bombardier went into the front turret to get the clearest and earliest possible view of whatever might be visible and useful to us in fixing our position.

"Almost at once we began flying in cloud, which was patchy in areas and a light-beacon was seen, which was flashing its identification letter, but only intermittently.

"There was some doubt at first as what letter was being flashed, but it was agreed on. Although, if what was reported was true, it made us fifty miles ahead of where my "dead-reckoning" put us. My own opinion of my navigation was such that this did not cause me such surprise. I forgot that useful maxim, "believe nothing you hear, and only half what you see", and agreed that we should now turn onto our course for base, and assured the pilots that it should be alright to keep on losing height through the cloud, which now completely enshrouded us, as we should be over the plains leading north to Yorkshire.

"Flying in cloud had a timeless quality, so I cannot even guess how long we continued to descend, but, when our altimeter showed 1400 feet, Carl decided to climb out of it, just in case we were not where we thought we were, but somewhere near higher ground.

"And then it happened.

"I was sitting on the floor, with my back to the bulkhead door of the pilots compartment; the wireless operator amazed me by beating his face on his set. I can remember thinking that being annoyed because the set would not function properly was one thing, but to vent one's rage by beating one's head on the thing was rather much.

"My attention was drawn to heather and herbage coming up through the floor, which did not seem consistent with flight through cloud, however thick, and then I realised that I had been sitting at my table, which was at an odd angle, that I did not recall leaving it, and that the motors no longer roared. There was a significant amount of crackling going on, together with the smell of hot oil and metal.

"Suddenly and simultaneously the W/OP, with bleeding face and I without a scratch,

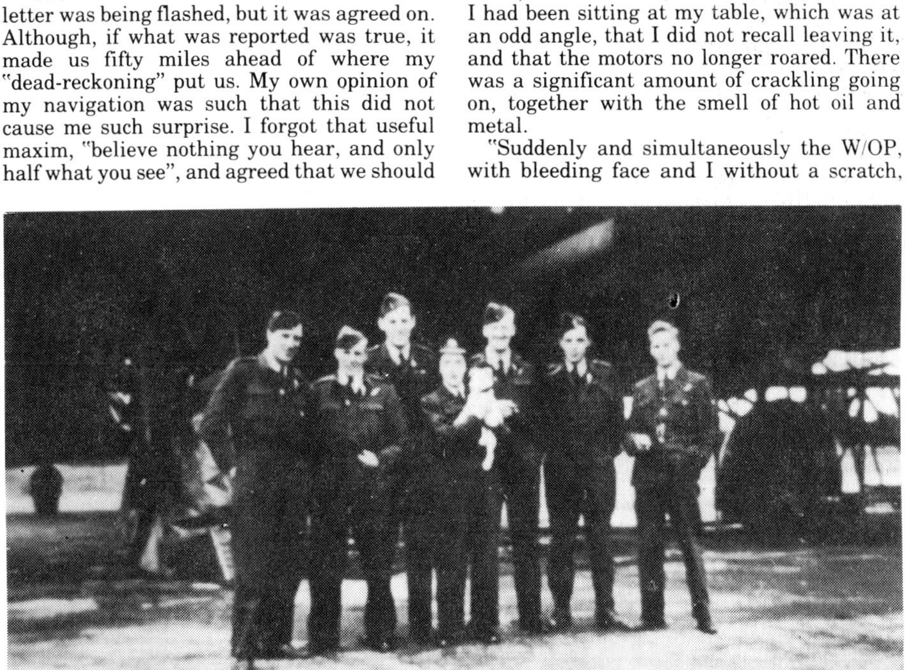

The crew after being posted to R.A.F. Leeming and re-equipped with Halifax B.V.'s. Here they have the addition of a flight engineer and a mid-upper gunner. Three of the original crew who crashed in Wellington X3348 are: second from left, D. Mortimer, bomb aimer; C. Taylor, pilot; D. Martin, navigator. The wireless operator, W. (Taffy) Baker, on the extreme right missed the Lorient raid and the resulting crash because of a heavy cold.

realised that we had crashed, and sitting around was no way to react. We both got moving towards the astrodome, which doubled as an escape hatch. I was surprised to meet another fellow there, for we only had a rear gunner, but such is the state of one's mind at such a time, that it did not occur to me that he too might be lookng for the exit!

"After what seemed tens of minutes, during which the crackling seemed ever more ominous, we got the hatch open and shot out of that hole like pips out of a gooseberry, to find the two pilots already out and getting organised on the rescue of the bombardier from the front turret.

"In all our minds was the fear of the sudden explosion into fire that usually accompanied such accidents as ours, and the problem of getting him out looked almost impossible to solve.

"The turret looked as if some giant had gripped it with one hand at the bottom and the other at the top and just wrung it like a dishcloth. What with the twisting, and the gun-breeches in there, the only evidence that were was room for a man as well was the presence of the man, unconscious but alive, and lying so oddly that it seemed he must be broken in many places.

"Still there was that crackling and fizzing from the motors — it was so dark, wet, and cold.

"I never did know, and never was able to recall, how we at last got him out. We worked in a sort of controlled frenzy trying not to hurry so much as to make his apparent injuries worse, yet not so slowly as to be caught halfway through the job by the expected fire. I know it occurred to us that if his legs were broken, it would make withdrawal easier, if only we could get a big enough gap to get his head and shoulders through.

"At last we did manage such a gap, and he was out. We carried him away from the threat of that crackling plane.

"Now the mist had cleared somewhat, and we could see the plane sitting on the ground in flying position, quite level. Also, as our frightened ears calmed down, we found that the noises were getting less and less threatening. Soon we were sure that the risk of fire was negligible when compared with the risk to Mortimer of exposure, so we returned to the plane and got him inside, wrapping him against the raw cold with what materials we could find.

"He was quite quiet, being, we supposed concussed and having apparently suffered severe leg injuries. Not that we probed too much, once we had made sure that he was not badly gashed anywhere.

"Where we were was anyone's guess, and we could see nothing nor hear anything. Someone had to stay with the injured bombaimer, someone had to go looking for help. We found that between the six of us we had just one torch to light our way back to civilization.

"Someone thought of the Very pistol, so, with my battledress pockets and blouse stuffed with cartridges, I and two others stood, deciding which way to head into the darkness to find help.

"Then we heard a train — most certainly the most welcome train there ever was, especially as we saw its fire. Since then I have been able to accept any coincidence. That blessed fireman decided to open his fire box and bung in another lump just at the right moment, for a noise can come from anywhere, but a pinpoint of light, in almost impenetrable blackness, comes from one place, and you can walk towards that place.

"I fired a Very cartridge to let us see the ground in our immediate path, and we set off. The light from that cartridge showed us little for our comfort; heather, and a soft brown peaty soil, with deep cuts in it, which made me worry about bogs.

"We set off, firing the pistol at intervals to light our way. At least when we fell over, which was often, with the heather and those little gullies, we fell softly.

The wireless operator, the rear gunner and myself made up the party. How we wished for another train, for it is hard to keep a straight path when no landmarks are visible. A Very cartridge gives only a little light, and that's not for long.

"Shortly, we came to an edge, and the earth seemed to go down suddenly. Several cartridges failed to show any sort of path, so over we went being as careful as we could, since we would not be much good with broken legs; somehow you feel that if you break your neck you will be excused, but breaking a leg is just silliness.

"So we tripped on rocks, fell into a stream, (it seemed like "streams", but turned out to be "a stream". We stumbled in cracks in the ground and just slithered on our backs or fronts or sides, whichever happened to be in contact with the ground when we fell, down the steepest bits.

"I have a genius for landing myself with much toil in the course of trying to dodge it, and even on this occasion managed to find time to practice.

"I found a broken down wall, and looking up from the glen, saw what I took to be a house gable on the skyline, so I climbed up to rouse the residents. Of course, it wasn't a house . . . it wasn't even a barn; it was just an odd arrangement of rock. So I slithered back down the glen and fell into that stream filling my trousers with water again, and found myself even beyond profanity.

"Fortunately the Very cartridges remained firable, and we three continued our descent with the aid of their feeble glimmers. At last we found a noticeable path, fields, and suddenly we were in a village.

"It was well past closing time, and being winter the people were abed. Our calls brought forth nobody and so we picked a door, and knocked firmly. After quite a noticeable interval did we get the welcome question 'Who are you?' from an upstairs window.

"Having announced our identities, in my cockney, backed up by the gunner's broad Durham accents our interrogator seemed satisfied that we were 'some of Our's' if you see what I mean. He opened up the door, took us in, sent someone to rally the village, and the local organization for the defence of the Realm.

"We were at a farm house in Hope-in-Edale, in Derbyshire, some fifty miles off our course.

"In no time flat the fire was kindled to a blaze, we all had a beer to tide us over till the kettle boiled. I was on the 'phone to our base, just in time to stop the "We regret to inform you that your son/husband/father/brother (or what have you) has failed to return from operations" telegrams going out. Also forstalling the consumption of six rum rations and bacon and eggs (homing bait) by anyone who happened to be nearest to them. At the same time a party was being assembled to go up to the moor to fetch Mortimer and the two pilots from the plane.

"Incidentally, in the course of converstion, we learned that our "arrival" had been heard, but past experience had taught our friends that going looking for survivors in the dark was usually a wasted effort. I think we were the first to "come visiting" so to speak.

"One of the assembling party was a local shepherd. Lean, weatherbeaten, slow of speech, calm mannered, quietly spoken, he examined us on our route down off the moor. We gave him as much detail as we could, (even to my misbegotten clump of rocks), and

American national Carl Taylor, checked out as unsuitable for flying by the U.S.A.A.F., proved his worth as a pilot in the R.A.F.

A recent photograph of Mr. Martin.

at the end he declared that he thought he knew of a path which would bring us up pretty well to the plane. So off we all went, the Pathfinder, with me right behind him, a stretcher party and a doctor.

"Our pace seemed very leisurely, though perhaps my judgment was faulted by a desire to get help to Mortimer as quickly as possible; in any case, I soon found that if I kept station with the leader, I would do very nicely.

"I suppose that was a path; all I did was watch where the shepherd put his feet, and put mine in the same places. After an age of plodding, we were up on the moor top, and looking round to try to pick out the plane in the blackness. I knew it was not much good me looking; when examined for my fitness for aircrew it was found there were insufficient grades of 'night-vision', so they crossed them all out and wrote 'poor'.

"The 'Locals', however soon picked out the unusual shadow that should not have been there, and vindicated the shepherd's confidence in his powers, for there was the Wimpy, no more than a hundred yards from us.

"The doctor's opinion of Mortimer's condition was encouraging and Morty's spirit now that he was nearly conscious, was also heartening, but what was even more heartening were his emphatic comments on our capacity as stretcher bearers as we bore him down that glen. It is a fact that had we not tied him on, he would have been in the village before us!

"Notwithstanding the apparent slowness of our travel, the trip up the glen and down again had taken only about an hour, and there to meet us on our return was an ambulance ready to take our more seriously injured straight to hospital. The local organisation was right on the ball. The local hotelier had hot baths and a meal and beds ready for us who were not so bent that Nature herself couldn't do the straightening. When we woke next morning, our clothes were dried, and there was good news of our fellow crashers in hospital.

"Don Mortimer had, incredibly, not broken any bones, but had severely twisted ankles. He still walks a bit awkwardly, compared with his quick athletic step before the accident, but he came back and finished a tour of ops. with us and then got shot down on his second tour, after qualifying as a pilot. Having seen him in that twisted turret, I think that this is one of the great marvels I have witnessed."

Out of the nine aircraft detailed from 427 Squadron, eight dropped their bombs on Lorient, from around 15,000 feet through 10/10 cloud. All made it back to England but had to land at various airfields due to lack of fuel.

Z for Zebra bounced along the only flat surface within ten miles when it struck the Derbyshire hills at Blackden Edge. The escape of all the crew members was considered so fortunate as to warrant a feature article in some Sunday newspapers, with headings 'Pilot makes miraculous landing — Million to one chance.'

Wellington X3348 was broken up and dragged off the moor — a few fragments remain at the site.

As for the target, the French town of Lorient, it, along with St. Naziare — was flattened. U-boats were to lie secure in their concrete pens until the following year when a bomb was developed that would penetrate the reinforced concrete.

The effects of those early raids on the Battle of the Atlantic amounted to giving U-boat crews some disturbed nights.

In May, 1943, 427 (Lion) Squadron R.C.A.F. was adopted by the Metro-Goldwyn-Mayer film company. Their first Halifax B.V.'s were named after M.G.M. stars. Towering above the adoption ceremony is DK 186 ZL-L, which was given the additional name 'Lana' after Lana Turner. One benefit for squadron members was free admission to M.G.M. films on show in London.

One Broken Jug

Republic Thunderbolt P47C "Flying Jug" COENEN

Thunderbolt P47C, 416227 of 63 Fighter Squadron USAAF, flying from Horsham St. Faith to Liverpool and return, crashed on Rushup Edge, April 25 1943. Map reference 093845.

It just did not make any sense to the fighter pilots who were to fly this, the latest production from Republic Aviation the P47 "Thunderbolt." It weighed six tons, looked big, fat and ugly to the American pilots who were used to the more sleekly-designed Airocobras, Lightnings and British Spitfires. Someone likened it to a jug — and the name stuck.

In April of 1943, a "Jug" of 56 Fighter Group, 8th Airforce, powerdived onto Rushup Edge, Edale, during a thunderstorm. The pilot, Second Lieutenant John E. Coenen, baled out, sustaining spinal damage, but went on — five months later — to destroy two German aircraft before being grounded and shipped back to the States because of his injuries.

The previous year, in July 1942, John E. Coenen had graduated as a fighter pilot at the age of 21 and after gaining experience on the new "pursuit airplane," he was assigned as a replacement pilot with 63 Fighter Squadron, 56 Fighter Group. The Group arrived in England on the Queen Elizabeth in January 1943.

In April, the Group was stationed at Horsham St. Faith, Norwich. Easter Sunday and some parts were required from Liverpool. Johnny "Fatboy" Coenen, who was Assistant Operations Officer with 63 Squadron volunteered to make the 180 mile trip across country.

As Coenen swung the heavy fighter's nose around to face the runway at Horsham, gusts of wind buffeted the Thunderbolt. It wasn't ideal flying weather on that Easter Sunday in 1943, but then the weather over England was rarely ideal.

In the three months of flying that Coenen and the other pilots of 56 Group had undergone, they had learned that if you didn't fly in adverse weather conditions you just didn't fly at all.

Coenen planned to fly to an airfield close to the city of Liverpool then borrow some motor transport to pick up the parts.

After an uneventful flight he reached his destination to discover that no transport was available — nor was public transport running because of the Bank Holiday. Coenen took off once more, heading for another airfield closer to his destination.

Towards evening he had the parts and was ready for the return trip — the weather was worsening. 2nd Lieutenant Coenen recalls what followed:—

"I tried to keep under the clouds but pretty soon they were right down on the hills in the

Manchester - Sheffield area. I decided to climb above the huge thunderheads which were piling up over the centre of England. I had started a normal climb and was right in among the thunderclouds when suddenly my plane began bucking and being tossed around like a cork on the ocean.

"I lost all sense of direction and at one point found myself hanging from my seat straps and realised that I was upside-down. The plane fell into a spin and I knew that under ideal conditions it took from 2 to 3,000 feet to pull a P47 out of a spin. I knew that I must be almost on top of the hills — I would never pull out in time. As far as I could see the plane was a gonner — I had to get out.

"Thrusting back the canopy and unstrapping myself, I stood up on the seat and attempted to jump — but found that I couldn't move; maybe the spin was responsible. I don't remember pulling the ripcord but I guess that I must have done, for I was torn away from the cockpit and looking up I could see the canopy opening up above me — one panel was missing and another torn — I was coming down pretty fast."

At Upper Booth in the Vale of Edale inhabitants were brought from their houses by a high-pitched roar in the rain-soaked skies. Bernard Taylor and his friends were out hiking that day and were sheltering from the storm in a house near Jacob's Ladder end of the valley. They ran out and were in time to hear the impact as the heavy fighter thudded into Dale Head — below Rushup Edge. They watched as a fire burned furiously at the crash site. The sound of exploding 0.50 ammuition echoed down the valley. Then, descending rapidly from the clouds the hikers spotted the pilot. Coenen hit — square on the path, landing awkwardly and heavily, then was dragged a short distance by his 'chute.

Mr. Taylor reached the pilot first — Coenen was groaning with pain. He asked the American to try to move his legs to see if his spine was damaged. Johnny Coenen knew that he was hurt pretty badly and wouldn't allow the hikers to move him.

Spotting a five-barred gate the hikers led by Mr. Taylor, took it off its hinges and used it as a stretcher to move the pilot into "Lee House."

Mr. Taylor, of Didsbury, Manchester, recalls the occasion:—

"We ascertained that the pilot was flying alone because anyone who may have baled out could have drifted onto the Kinder Scout

plateau, a most inhospitable place on a stormy night like that. After making him as comfortable as possible we chased down to the Church House at Edale and telephone the police at Hope. Next morning we climbed across to the crash site — the fighter had buried itself with the impact into the side of the hill. The ground was littered with exploded shells or cartridges."

Johnny Coenen had fractured the 11th and 12th dorsal vertabrae of his backbone. Four and a half months later the pilot from Oklahoma returned to his Squadron, a part of 56 Group, to see some action — up to the time of the crash he had only flown one short sortie over the Dutch estuaries.

During practice flying he was experiencing some pain in his back especially when he pulled the "jug" into a tight turn. The pain could become so intense that it caused him to break formation more than once. Breaking a tight formation was considered a dangerous procedure when in action with the Luftwaffe, for it meant leaving the protective covering of your own fighters. Johnny Coenen put the pain down to weak muscles and he exercised daily to try and put matters right.

During the Spring and Summer of 1943, the Americans had stepped up their daylight deep penetrations bomber raids into Europe and the losses of the "Mighty Eighth" mounted. Steps were afoot to provide the Flying Fortresses and the Liberators with fighter cover. On September 27th, Thunderbolt fighters were to escort the "heavies" right to the target area to fight off the swarms of FW190's and Me.109's.

The target was Emden in the German homeland, which meant that the fighters faced a 200 miles journey over the North Sea. The trip was made possible by the use of 75 gallon drop tanks. Coenen's Squadron was to be part of this escort shepherding the second Task Force and on that September morning the weather was what the Americans had come to expect — cloudy and overcast.

The fighters climbed to 24,000 feet and set out to rendezvous with the B17's off the Frisian Islands. Because of the rapidly deteriorating weather conditions the fighters of 56 Group failed to make contact with their charges.

It was only after the bombers had completed the raid on Emden that the Thunderbolts picked them up and took up protective positions. Coenen was positioned last in a box of four fighters of 63 Squadron — they were far out to the right of the B17's. This position placed Coenen in the extreme rear. As the raiders headed out over the sea, Coenen was the last man out of Germany. This was his

2nd Lieutenant John Coenen posed in typical fighter pilot stance.

13th mission since returning to his Squadron and it was to be his last.

They were at 24,000 feet when Coenen's flight leader, Captain Vogt, spotted some unidentified aircraft below them. These appeared to be heading towards the B17's. Leading his flight of four "jugs" Captain Vogt descended to investigate. The aircraft were single-engined fighters — six of them — radial engines . . .Focke-Wulf 190's. As Vogt started into a turning circle with the six. Coenen spotted nine more coming in from the left. The odds were 4 to 1 against the Americans — they needed help.

Attempts to bring assistance from some of the other P47's of 56 Squadron were thwarted by some effective jamming of the Allied radios by German ground control.

Johnny Coenen found himself suffering increasing pain in his back as he was forced to push hard on the rudder pedal to keep formation in the turning circle with the more manoeuvrable FW190's. The torture became unbearable — on the point of passing out he broke away to the opposite side of the circle — usually a fatal manoeuvre — but he could not help himself.

With the fighter trimmed for turns, immediately he broke away, the nose shot up and the FW's began to turn inside him intent upon making him their first victim.

Seeing Coenen's plight, Vogt and Number 2, pitched in to the FW's closing in on Coenen. Number 3 was not seen to go down to the FW's, but he must have been hit first, for none of the others saw him again after they broke the circle to assist Coenen.

For Coenan the pain lessened as he levelled off at 25,000 feet, but the nippy German fighters had stayed with him and were closing in for the kill.

Suddenly, a FW appeared in front of him — the German pilot must have misjudged his speed in his eagerness to score. It was an opportunity Coenen wasn't going to miss — having resigned himself to being shot down he

had decided to try and "throw a little lead" before they got him.

Realising his mistake, the German pilot began to turn into the Thunderbolt but in doing so provided an excellent target. Coenen's first burst hit the fuselage down the left side. The eight 0.50 machine guns put up a devastating fuselade and he watched in wonder as his second burst sprayed along both wings taking in the cockpit.

The pilot must have been hit for the FW settled back and took no evasive action as Coenen closed in and set it aflame with a further burst.

As could happen in dogfights of the Second World War, one minute a particular part of the sky could be filled with aircraft fighting and twisting in a general melee and the next minute hardly any aircraft in sight.

He had watched his victim trailing smoke as the FW dropped in a steady spin through the clouds at 5,000 feet below — now he was alone.

Above him in the distance he spotted the unmistakeable bulks of two Thunderbolts — if he could tag on to them he might stand a chance of getting home.

As he began to overhaul them he noted another radial-engined fighter apparently intent upon catching the two P47 Thunderbolts ahead — only this one — sporting a bright yellow nose — was a preying FW190. The eerie whining whistle in his earphones told Coenen that the Germans were still jamming — he had no way of warning the two American fighters.

Coenen glanced around to make sure there were no other German fighters closing in on him — and finding himself clear he opened up the throttle.

The Thunderbolt was notoriously slow off the mark because of the enormous size — but once it got moving the speed built up gradually until it could overhaul any German fighter then flying. Within minutes Coenen had caught up to the stalking FW190, the pilot of which was too intent on bagging his two fat prey to notice the Thunderbolt tucked in out of sight under the FW's condensation trail.

At 75 yards, Coenen squeezed the trigger on the control column and the fighter in his sights "lit up like a Christmas Tree." It fell earthwards, the German pilot making no attempt to get out.

Coenen felt a surge of satisfaction as he recognised the code letters on the two unsuspecting Thunderbolts — It was Vogt and his No. 2 — he had returned the favour . . .

That day 63 Fighter Squadron had five victories — the Number 3 in Coenen's flight was the only casualty. The Thunderbolts of 56 Group had flown 400 miles, mostly over water, and inflicted a defeat of 21 to 1 on the enemy. Two of the enemy had fallen to 2nd Lieutenant John E Coenen, but his elation was shortlived when he was grounded because of his spinal injuries . . sustained when the dropped out of the skies over Derbyshire. He was awarded the Air Medal and two clusters, but then was sent home to recuperate.

Small scraps to be found on the surface.

Flying Bomb USN

Liberator PB4Y-1 63934, of VB110 Bombing Squadron, United States Navy, Dunkeswell, returning from Bay of Biscay patrol, abandoned by the crew over Lincolnshire, crashed at Broken Ground, December 18, 1943. Map reference 006018.

It was a particularly bad night as Mr. Utton walked along the blacked - out road from Stalybridge to Millbrook. It was going on for 9 o' clock — just seven days before Christmas 1943.

Above the wind, he heard the sound of an aeroplane approaching from the south west and flying along the valley in his direction — it sounded low.

Suddenly, a huge, black shape — darker than the surrounding night, roared into view passing a mere 300 feet above the chimneys of Hartshead Power Station. Mr. Utton stared after it in amazement as it lumbered on up the valley — did the crew realise how low they were? Did they know of the high ground lying directly ahead of them? It seemed to him that something was seriously wrong. Had he been able to see aboard the four-engined bomber, he would have been even more surprised — and alarmed.

Tucked into the bomb bay of the PB4Y-1 (Consolidated Liberator) of the United States Navy were 16 depth charges each consisting of 250 lbs. of torpex high explosive.

Nothing stirred within the ponderous, box-shaped fuselage — every crew position was unoccupied — including the 1st and 2nd pilots' positions. The anti - submarine bomber was deserted and flying on automatic pilot. A wrecked radar set was the only damage — this had been deliberately destroyed by a small explosive charge. Fuel gauges on the pilot's instrument panel were registering zero and had been for the past fifteen minutes or so. The starboard outer engine had been the first to falter and stop. With no pilot's hand to press the feathering button, the huge propeller continued to turn causing sufficient drag to pull the doomed bomber off its pre-set course, thus causing it to turn away from the heavily populated area of Lancashire.

Who had set that lethal flying bomb lumbering across industrial England — and why?

It was fourteen hours earlier, at 07.00 that PB4Y-1 63934 took off from RAF Dunkeswell in Devon for a routine patrol over the Bay of Biscay. At the controls was Lieutenant George Charno United States Naval Reserve — beside him in the 2nd pilot's seat was the co-pilot, Robert G. Wissman, a lieutenant junior grade. Along with them were eight other crew members plus a passenger, a total of eleven USN flyers.

Four other PB4Y-1's of Bombing Squadron 110 were on anti - submarine patrol that morning of December 18th. None of them would make it back to their base at Dunkeswell. Bombing Squadron 110 had just two months earlier become a part of the Battle of the Atlantic, which had had its beginnings three years previously when the German Reich announced a total blockade of the British Isles on August 17th, 1940. England was to be starved into submission by cutting off her sea links with the USA. This cutting off was to be accomplished by Admiral Donitz's U-boats.

With the fall of France, the Kriegsmarine secured bases in the Bay of Biscay from where they could sail to intercept the massive convoys of merchant ships crossing the Atlantic. By mid-1942, the U-boats were gaining the upper hand as they hunted and attacked in packs. Battles would last for days and sometimes it meant destruction for a particular convoy.

The tide of the Battle of the Atlantic turned in 1943 when long-range aircraft were used in greater numbers — equipped with radar they began to locate and sink U-boats in increasing numbers.

The Bay of Biscay was an ideal location to catch the submarines as they set out from, or returned to their concrete pens at Brest, St. Nazaire and Lorient. It was here that Coastal Command — operating from bases in southern England — tried to force them to stay submerged, thus decreasing the endurance of the batteries and men, making the U-boats less effective in the shipping lanes. During the summer of 1943, 20 U-boats had been destroyed in the Bay of Biscay. However, RAF Coastal Command was under pressure from the Luftwaffe operating from airfields in Brittany. Help was on its way in the form of USN anti-submarine units. In July 1943, in the United States, a new Squadron was being formed — it was to be designated "Patrol Squadron VB-110". Among its pilots — who volunteered to be a part of that new Squadron — was Joe Kennedy, elder brother of the late John F. Kennedy, who was to become a President of the United States.

On the trip across the Atlantic to the UK,

Joe Kennedy's plane and the crew of 63934, piloted by Charno kept company — arriving at St. Eval in Cornwall via Greenland. After completing acclimatisation, 110 Squadron moved to Dunkeswell in Devon and was ready for operations against German submarines.

Patrols were up to twelve hours long and were most uncomfortable for the crews. Towards the rear of the PB4Y it was icy cold and yet in the cockpit it could become like an oven. Meals on the long patrols consisted of coffee and sandwiches eaten with the crew scouring the skies for German fighters and the ocean for U-boats. By December the flying weather was appalling and Dunkeswell lay in a covering of snow. But the constant patrols seemed to be keeping the U-boats beneath the surface in the Bay of Biscay; so when the weather was good enough at dawn for take-off, regardless of the evening forecast, the patrols set out. When the weather worsened the returning planes landed where they could.

On the morning of December 18th, at 4 a.m., George Charno joined his co-pilot in the freezing aerology hut along with Joe Kennedy and three other pilots with their co-pilots. Five aircraft were to go on patrol over "U-boat Alley". They listened as the weather officer predicted a cold front moving in from the west, that would more than likely close Dunkeswell at around 5.30, when they were due for return.

Despite this information, there was no move made to scrub the operation and eventually the crews filed into the flight mess for the traditional pre-flight breakfast of steak and eggs.

At 07.00 hours it was still dark as the pilot lifted the PB4Y from the runway and pointed its nose to the west. The Cornish coastline passed beneath them and the navigator gave the course change that would place them at their assigned patrol area "percussion T-4" over the Bay. The weather was atrocious, with the clouds down to 400 feet in places and winds gusting at 50 knots. Visibility was bad and adding to the crews' lack of vision was the heavy condensation forming on the aircraft's cockpit plexiglass.

George Charno opted to carry out the patrol at 1500 feet up in the overcast. The probing radar beam would pick up anything moving on the ocean's surface in their area.

Patrolling another alloted section of the Bay, Joe Kennedy began his search below the cloud and was forced into wave-hopping as the gale force wind whipped the waves into a near-storm.

The morning dragged on for the pilot and his crew until 1100 when a radio message was received from 19th Group back at Dunkeswell, informing them that the expected bad weather front was moving in to the British Isles faster than earlier predicted. All five patrolling PB4Y's were to return to base by 1700.

The pilot of 63934 had been expecting that recall and made no change in the patrol — and so completed one circuit of it.

On the return trip, the weather seemed to improve as they neared the Cornish coast; but they could see coming in behind them a huge bad weather front. Dunkeswell lay shrouded in heavy overcast and it was drizzling with rain. With visibility down to 1400 yards, the controller decided to divert the five returning U-boat hunters to RAF Beaulieu near Southampton.

PB4Y 63934 made landfall at Bude Bay and dropped low enough to keep visual contact with the ground — it was a straight run home. Their flight path took them over Winkleigh Airfield but as they had received no communication that their Base at Dunkeswell was "out" they continued.

Whilst still homing on the radio beacon at Dunkeswell they received the order to divert to Beaulieu some 75 miles to the east, in a direct line. Passing over their base the co-pilot suggested that they could put down at home — although conditions were not the best. However, Charno reasoned that Beaulieu must be clear and safe — why take chances landing in difficult conditions?

Anyway, they had received their orders.

The navigator, Ensign Cecil R. Colyer, altered course for Beaulieu and the radioman changed frequency to pick up that airfield. He then requested from Beaulieu altimeter setting and cloud base.

Visibility was becoming increasingly reduced as heavy condensation began to build up and darkness fell. The pilot pulled the PB4Y up to 1500 feet and flew on instruments, arriving over Beaulieu at 1700 hours.

The approach had been frustrating for as they were coming in towards the field on what was known as a QGH (this was a procedure for bringing in aircraft in unfavourable conditions). Radio messages were five minutes late in arriving because of communications congestion from other aircraft. But, at last they were in a position to begin landing procedure according to the message they were receiving.

63934 dropped through the cloud base to 800 feet — no sign of landing lights!

"Turn back west — we've missed the field," called the wireless operator.

Cursing, the pilot dipped the port wing and began to turn back on a westerly heading.

PB4Y-1 taking off on anti-submarine patrol.

U.S. NATIONAL ARCHIVES

"Barrage balloons!" yelled co-pilot Robert Wissman.

A low whistle in their earphones signalled the truth of his warning — they were roaring through a vast forest of balloon cables and picking up their avoidance signals.

"Must be Southampton," muttered Charno as he turned the bomber south and headed away from the danger area.

The radio was crackling and spluttering as hail and rain lashed the aircraft. Over the air, frantic calls of other planes could be heard as they tried to establish their positions.

The co-pilot added his voice to the melee — informing Flying Control at Beaulieu that they had been in the air over 12 hours and were running short on gas. The cockpit seemed to crowd in on the two pilots and the temperature was climbing higher — the windows ran with condensation.

Another radio signal from Flying Control — should they try another blind approach on their radio beam?

"Let's make for the south coast — I think I can find the field myself once I know exactly where we are," snapped Wissman.

Ignoring the radio signals they continued south. Suddenly, they were at the coast and with every crew member peering earthwards they fixed their position.

"Portsmouth!" came a triumphant cry.

"Leave it to me!" called the co-pilot as he took over the controls. With the starboard wing well down the co-pilot stared out into the gloom and picked up the Isle of Wight; sticking to the coastline he flew to the northern - most tip then crossed the Solent.

"Keep your eyes peeled for the inlet of river Beaulieu!" he called to the men who where peering through the nose.

They contacted Flying Control again: "We are having difficulty locating the field on QDM's — for Pete's sake, turn on the aerodrome lights!" yelled the pilot.

Coolly came back the reply from Beaulieu, "All runway lights are on. . ."

In the bomber they could see nothing through the rain squalls. Once they picked up the river mouth it should have been easy — Beaulieu airfield lay a short way to the west about two miles up the inlet. At least they now knew where they were as they followed the river; however, they received a signal informing them that there was an obstruction ahead of them — and a safe altitude was suggested.

"Incredible!" gasped Wissman as he pulled back on the controls, taking the bomber up into the overcast.

"That does it — how are we supposed to get down?"

"We'll try on QDM — again. We'll let Flying Control get us down," said the pilot, taking over once more.

"Initiate QDM letdown procedure," he called to his radioman.

"We've been instructed to wait — there are other planes on this circuit," replied the radioman — the irritation in his voice was all-too apparent as he manipulated his spluttering apparatus.

The two pilots began to calculate their remaining flying time and concluded that they had sufficient for three hours. It was about

1800 hours and now completely dark.

They continued flying on a northerly heading for a short time and then began flying on alternate east and west headings — timing their flight in order to maintain a position just north of Beaulieu.

"OK! It's our turn!" yelled the radioman. "Beaulieu wish to commence QGH procedure with us — go to 1,700 feet."

The pilot dropped gently through the clouds and froze — balloon warning whistles filled his earphones . . . He turned immediately 090 but didn't dare climb for fear of colliding with one of the other planes circling above.

"I can't hold the signal!" the radioman called, his voice filled with urgency. He was having difficulty tuning the transmitter. It was pointless carrying on with an airfield approach — and Charno recommenced flying alternate east and west headings.

The smell of the overheated transmitter filled the cockpit. What with weather playing havoc with the antennae, and constant, frantic use the wireless transmitter was getting, it was little wonder that it was beginning to pack in. Using the command set, the pilot began to employ the "darky" system (code name for emergency R.T. organisation for assistance) and succeeded in getting an answer — but it was unreadable. He, the co-pilot and the navigator listened on the command set and continued to call "darky" for the remainder of the flight but received no answer.

They were in serious trouble: they turned their IFF (Identification Friend or Foe) system to "Emergency!"

"We have Beaulieu again and they are recommending a QGH," called the radioman.

"This is it . . . we're going in and to hell with the balloons!" called Charno who was convinced that they were far enough away from the Southampton area to worry about the warning whistles.

"It's gone, it's gone!" cried the radioman as he desperately twiddled the knobs on the transmitter. "It's conked out!"

It was 18.30 hours.

At about that time, Joe Kennedy swept in through the wind and rain, aided by flares, and put his PB4Y down at Beaulieu aerodrome. As he taxied his weary aircraft and crew off the runway, the control tower was sending up flares to try to help 63934.

At one point, the crew thought they saw flares — but were unable to develop the sightings.

When it became obvious that the radio would never work again, the pilot once more let down through the overcast and ordered the crew to keep look-out through the two after hatches. They were to watch for airfield lights, searchlights, anything that would help them pinpoint their position.

"Lights!" came the cry from the co-pilot's seat.

Sure enough a long, straight stretch of twin lights lay beneath them . . .

"It's got to be a runway!" called the co-pilot hopefully. Charno lined up the lights and began an approach.

"Climb!" screamed a voice on the intercom. "For Pete's sake . . . climb!"

Without asking for an explanation — (the urgency in the navigator's yell didn't encourage questions) Charno once again pushed the throttles open and powered for the clouds.

"Convoy — it was a convoy of army lorries," the navigator cried hoarsely. "We must have scared 'em half to death!"

"They're not the only ones", was the thought that echoed through the bomber.

They were running low on fuel, the weather was worsening, they didn't know precisely their position and the radio was out. There was nothing left for them to do but bale out. Charno spiralled to 5,000 feet above the position they had last seen the trucks. Well above the clouds they headed in a northerly direction.

None of the crew had ever jumped before and from a height of 5,000 feet they continued to peer at the rainswept earth below, praying for runway lights.

At 19.45 hours, the pilot gave the order to destroy the radar gear. The navigator organised the crew and hurriedly but calmly gave instructions. They were scared and the inevitable happened — one of the crew yanked at his ripcord and his 'chute filled the after-station with silk. His buddies bundled it up again and stuffed it into his arms — this was no time for niceties.

At 20.00 hours, the navigator reported that the crew was ready to jump. The crewman with the "unpacked" chute was the first to go, as his fellow airmen pushed him out — the others quickly following. At 20.15 all hands in the after station had gone out through the tunnel hatch.

Wissman ducked down into the nose and dropped through the nosewheel door into the night.

It had been a bad day. And it wasn't over yet — the pilot had still one job to do — detonate the IFF equipment. He would have to put the plane on automatic pilot, explode the IFF — and jump.

Turning the plane on a heading of 290 degrees, the automatic pilot was set, the secret equipment destroyed and then the pilot left through the nosewheel door.

The whole crew landed in Lincolnshire, and apart from some scratches and bruises, they were all right. They were 150 miles north of their intended landing place and a short distance from the Wash. Meanwhile, the empty, depth charge - laden bomber droned on across the centre of England with sufficient potential in its belly to destroy a whole town centre. Just short of Manchester, the last dregs of fuel were burned up in the starboard outer Twin Wasp radial engine and it spluttered into silence. The automatic pilot, unable to compensate for the enormous amount of drag produced by the windmilling prop, permitted the flying bomb to enter a terminal clockwise circuit — losing height gradually, it thundered along the Tame River Valley. Workers at Hartshead Power Station rushed out in time to see the huge roaring black shape almost scrape the station's chimneys before it was swallowed up in the wintry night.

With speed reducing constantly, the PB4Y still turning to starboard, crossed over the town of Mossley and thudded into the hard grit covered moor known as Broken Ground, some 1500 feet above sea level. There was no fire — there was no fuel left to burn. Because of the relatively soft crash landing, the high explosives failed to go off despite the fact that the jolt had caused the depth charges to tumble from the bomb bay onto the moor.

The following day, local people went up to the Moors to examine the American bomber. Mr. John Mason (who was 38 years old at the time and the gamekeeper for that stretch of moorland) kept guard over the wreck all through the following night. But when a team of USA servicemen arrived, they seemed less conscientious. It wasn't long before some of the locals had stripped the plane of valuable articles — the transmitter was the first to go. A demolition team exploded the depth charges. Later, PB4Y-1 63934 was broken up by a local man and sold for scrap. A few of the heavier objects remained at the site.

Charno of PB4Y 63934 was commended by the Commander Fleet Air Wing Seven, Commodore Hamilton, for "Taking correct and decisive action in an emergency and for the obvious good discipline of the crew." What would have happened if the starboard engine had kept running just two or three minutes' longer can only be guessed at. Or if the port outer had packed in first — the results would have been the same: that the crewless bomber would have been circuiting Stockport and

A USAAF Liberator in the same position that PB4Y-1 63934, USN ended up in after it made a relatively 'soft' crash landing at Broken Ground. VIA DAVID SMITH

Manchester, gradually losing height with no possibility of a soft deposit for its lethal cargo.

It is interesting to note that six months later, the Americans were to formulate a plan to use an explosive - packed PB4Y to attack the enemy — German V weapon sites on the French coast were to be the targets and a special force SAU-1 (Special Attack Unit) was formed at Dunkeswell. It was a volunteer force and the volunteers were crews from VB-110 Navy Squadron. Among the first to volunteer was Lieutenant Joe Kennedy, son of the former US Ambassador to Britain, Joseph P. Kennedy.

Joe Jnr. had seen his younger brother John F. Kennedy, win fame as a Navy Motor Torpedo Boat Commander in the Pacific — a naval hero who had saved his crew when his boat was chopped in two by a Japansese destroyer. Unable to score himself in the anti-submarine war in the Atlantic, Joe Jnr. scorned a proffered desk job and volunteered to fly a worn-out PB4Y packed with 21,170 lbs. of Torpex towards the enemy coast. The plan was for him to take the flying bomb off the ground — put it on course for the target, set the arming solenoid, then bale out near Dover. Another aircraft would guide the pilotless bomb on to the target by remote control.

On August 12th, 1944, the mission began but whilst the bomber was still over England, it mysteriously blew up — tragically killing Joe Kennedy and his co-pilot "Bud" Willy.

By the end of the war, Navy Squadron VB110 at Dunkeswell had lost sixty - eight men killed. Two aircraft were lost to enemy fighters whilst on anti-submarine patrol over the Bay of Biscay; ten aircraft were lost to mechanical failure and bad weather — the remains of just one of these lies on Broken Ground at the edge of the Peak District.

Undercarriage legs and an engine block along with metal scraps are all that remain today.

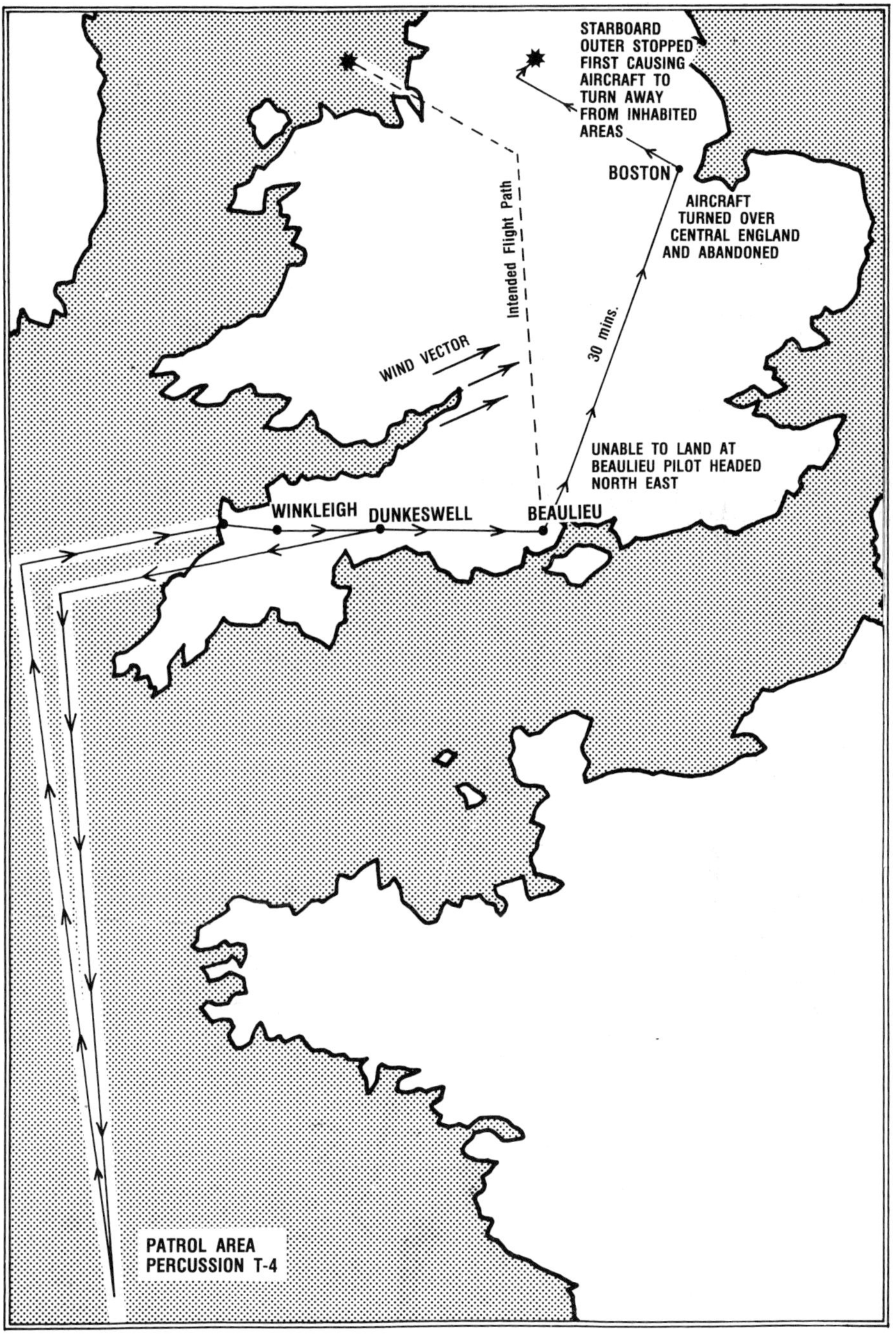
STARBOARD OUTER STOPPED FIRST CAUSING AIRCRAFT TO TURN AWAY FROM INHABITED AREAS
BOSTON
AIRCRAFT TURNED OVER CENTRAL ENGLAND AND ABANDONED
Intended Flight Path
30 mins.
WIND VECTOR
UNABLE TO LAND AT BEAULIEU PILOT HEADED NORTH EAST
WINKLEIGH
DUNKESWELL
BEAULIEU
PATROL AREA PERCUSSION T-4

The Lost Summer

Spitfire P7883 of 53 Operational Training Unit, Hibalstow, practising formation flying, crashed above Barber Booth, December 10, 1943. Map reference 110837.

The hospital ward looked strange and different to the young Flight Sergeant as he slowly opened his eyes. A throbbing pain in his head reminded him of what he was doing there — a head-on crash with another Spitfire — but there was something still not quite right. There was a dreamlike quality about the whole situation — as if he had been asleep for a long time.

The beds were different — he seemed to be facing the wrong wall and there were strange faces around him.

He decided that they must have moved him during the night. But something else was puzzling him: his injuries, his amazing escape from the blazing Spitfire which crash-landed heavily had left him with two fractured legs, a fractured spine, a broken nose and one broken arm. And yet, some of his injuries seemed to have healed remarkably quickly. Maybe, he reasoned, he had suffered some sort of a relapse. Perhaps he was emerging from a coma?

The last thing he could remember was lying in a hospital bed at Larbart in Scotland, however the nurse had just informed him that he was in a hospital in Buxton, Derbyshire — over two hundred miles away in the South.

Outside the windows he could see that it was wintertime — people around him were discussing Christmas and yet it should have been Easter. What, he wondered, had happened to the summer of 1943?

"You've been involved in an accident," the nurse kindly explained. "You crashed in your Spitfire."

"Yes, I know," he replied. Ron Mitchell, the young pilot still felt his mind was in chaos. Nothing seemed to make sense. He was in the wrong place . . . at the wrong time . . . and even more disturbing, with the wrong injuries.

That evening, he received a visit from his father and at last the truth began to emerge. At first his conversation with his father seemed to be all at cross-purposes.

"You crashed twice — not once. Don't you remember?"

Flight Lieutenant David Crichton was the RAF Doctor who had been involved in the fighter pilot's rescue from the Derbyshire moorland. This Officer was the pioneer of the Mountain Rescue Service. Stationed at RAF Harpur Hill, Buxton, the Doctor was in the thick of it when it came to high ground crashes. It was this Officer who began to fill in the missing gaps for Ron Mitchell. Seven months missing from his life . . .

In March, 1943, Ron Mitchell had been stationed at Grangemouth in Scotland at 53 Operational Training Unit — after returning from Canada where he had trained as a pilot.

On the afternoon of March 18th he took off in a Spitfire Mk1B to practise some formation flying — he could recall the details vividly. He formated on the port side of the flight leader in the number three position and on a line with him was another Spitfire, in the starboard position to the leader, at number two position. Behind and over to the right of number two, bringing up the rear, was number four. The idea was to try to hold formation on the leader, the Chief Flying Instructor — while he seemed hell-bent on ridding himself of his three fledglings. This was known as "tail-chasing."

They began a steep climb up through some heavy cumulus clouds. Ron Mitchell watched as the newer model Spitfire of the leader began to pull away. It was all right for the Instructor tearing upwards like that — but his trainees in the older Mk1s were struggling to keep up. He had the throttle wide open and was watching the speedo creep back until it reached 160 mph.

Glancing up from his instrument panel he froze! A dark shape was hurtling down out of the clouds towards him. He had time to identify the rapidly growing shape of another Spitfire — a split second before it rammed his port side with a mighty bang. Engine cowling whipped away in the slipstream and the huge black hulk of his Rolls-Royce Merlin reared up at him as it ripped free of its mountings and plunged away earthwards.

Flames shot from the 48 gallon fuel tank situated directly in front of the windshield and the stricken fighter went into a spin.

With the engine gone the centre of gravity moved back drastically. To offset the weight shift, Ron Mitchell pushed the control column hard forward and pulled back the cockpit canopy. He would have to get out for there was little hope of putting the Spitfire down in one piece . . . The aircraft was falling through cloud and beginning to go into a series of turns. Through the smoke and fumes sweeping past the cockpit, Ron could see some houses below — he was above a built-up area. That decided him. He had regained a little control but still could not prevent the turning so he would stay with it and attempt to put it down where it would do least harm.

An open space — a recreation ground presented itself. He managed to nudge the spiralling plane towards it.

The next thing he remembered he was sitting in the cockpit — all movement had ceased and the flames were beginning to break through the instrument panel . . . Co-ordination between his arms and his brain did not exist — he couldn't move, strapped in as he was, he would be cooked where he sat and he began to despair.

Suddenly, strong arms were working around him. Unfastening buckles and pulling back straps. Through the haze he could make out the blue uniform of a navy Petty Officer and the outline of another man. The man, who turned out to be a farm labourer, lifted him bodily from the blazing coffin and carried him to safety. The Spitfire was gutted.

He could recall that the pilot who had struck his aircraft was a trainee fighter pilot from the same Unit. He had made no apparent attempt to leave his aircraft and had been killed.

"What do you remember after that?" prompted Dr. Crichton.

The hospital, his injuries, convalescence . . . it began to come back . . . but nothing of the months since then. He was suffering from a severe case of amnesia after receiving a bang on the head from a second crash which had left a wrecked Spitfire close to the "Lord's Seat" on Rushup Edge, Derbyshire.

Additionally to the blow on the head, Ron had suffered a fractured arm and leg, plus frostbite.

To aid his full recovery, the RAF Doctor began to fill in the blanks in the young pilot's life. He was told that he had been in a flight of four Spitfires when he had informed his leader that he had run out of fuel — then dropping out of formation he had simply disappeared.

At Hibalstow, the satellite field for Kirton-in-Lindsey, the Flying Control Liaison Officer had made intensive enquiries of all the airfields in the vicinity, without success. The Royal Observer Corps were asked if they had spotted the errant Spitfire, but they were unable to help. The Police were requested to make inquiries and squadrons of number four Bomber Group were contacted with a view to searching the desolate hills of the Pennines. However, bad weather and overcast skies made an air search impossible at first.

Flying Officer Hawkins, the Flight Leader, made a brave attempt to take up his Spitfire and make an airsearch beginning with the approximate position where Mitchell's Spitfire disappeared. They had been off course at the time so it was difficult knowing where to begin and with no break in the weather, he had been forced to return.

During the following day (Saturday), Halifax bombers roared low over the Pennines with many eyes scanning through cloud gaps. As the Bombers had been "stood down" from operations because it was a period of full moon, aircraft in plenty were available to join in the search. During the day a bomber crew caught a glimpse of wreckage but then lost it in the overcast. A fix was obtained, however, and the approximate location passed on to the police who organised a further search with the help of the Home Guard.

Ron Mitchell

In the grey light of the full moon, the search parties scoured the hills but at around 0200 hours in typical moorland manner, clouds suddenly descended and the search had to be abandoned as the searchers themselves were in danger of becoming lost.

Just as the searchers were turning for base, on that freezing December night, a civilian helper stumbled upon some wreckage. The news was passed to the police and the RAF Mountain Rescue team led by Dr. Crichton raced through the night with an ambulance.

Wreckage was widespread, both wings had been ripped off as the fighter had bounced across the moor. The engine was located, then some distance further on the main fuselage.

The cockpit was empty — a parachute lay on the seat — at least the pilot hadn't baled out. He had been well enough to unstrap himself and climb out of the wreckage. There was blood about, however, so the pilot was obviously injured.

On the port side of the fuselage, just aft of the wireless equipment, a hinged panel gave access to a first aid kit — this had been opened and bandages removed. The pilot had been fit enough to treat himself but that had been over 36 hours ago. Alone and injured on desolate moorland in the middle of winter, the young pilot stood little chance of survival. Army units were brought in and every inch of the moor was systematically covered until, on Sunday lunchtime, a party discovered a figure crouched up in a dip in the ground

After 48 hours on the moorland, the unconscious, injured young pilot was transported to Buxton Cottage Hospital — and it was now December 12th, 1943. Ron Mitchell suffered loss of memory — as if the period between his first crash, his recovery and his return to flying had never happened . . . the two accidents had blurred into one in his confused mind. It was only gradually and slowly over many weeks that his memory began to return. Like pieces in a jigsaw, one bit of information linked to another until finally, and with the help of Dr. Crichton, he had the complete picture.

The four Spitfires that had set out on the Friday had been doing a practice reconnaissance down the East coast — there was no gap in the cloud. Ron Mitchell was tagging along in his 2½ year old Spitfire Mk V in the number four position. They were flying at 4000 feet and well above the low cloud base, travelling at 230 miles per hour. The flight of four had been travelling for 30 minutes when

Pilots of 611 Fighter Squadron in the Summer of 1944 when the Squadron was engaged in chasing Flying Bombs. Ron Mitchell is at the back, centre.

suddenly, Ron's engine coughed and went into a series of splutters.

Immediately, he pushed the fuel gauge button, which, incredibly, was registering nought. The tanks must not have been filled after the last flight — but the fuel gauge had not indicated this so it must have been faulty.

He informed Flying Officer Hawkins of his plight as he watched the other three planes pull away from him. Then, quickly he called base and asked for a homing course — and received course 090. He commenced to turn, losing height all the time.

"During my descent, I was not unduly perturbed at making a forced landing as that morning's briefing had been for us to fly courses above cloud over Lincolnshire — and to keep within reason near to the East Coast. The cloud was at 1000 feet and I had every chance of making a safe landing — wheels up."

The numerous airfields in Lincolnshire should have made it easy enough for him to find a field and put down safely. But the truth was that they were seventy miles off course — and over the treacherous peaks of Derbyshire.

He could remember entering the cloud but to this day, the crash, his survival on the moors for two days and nights, plus thirteen days in Buxton Cottage Hospital, remain a complete blank.

In six months time he was flying again, having fully recovered from his injuries — and in August of 1944 he joined 611 Fighter Squadron at Bradwell Bay in Essex. This was the summer of 1944, the period when Hitler unleashed his pilotless flying bombs against Southern England. Equipped with Spitfire IXs, 611 Squadron commenced anti "Diver" operations, chasing the V1s and bringing them down in unpopulated areas.

After a three month period in Scotland at the close of the year, 611 returned to the south to take up a new role — daylight bomber escort duties.

In February, the Squadron was equipped with long-range Mustang IVs and the following month Ron Mitchell took part in his last engagement with the enemy, making RAF history. 611 Squadron was the first RAF fighter squadron to meet the Soviet Air Force over Germany.

As the Second World War drew to its close with Hitler's Empire being crushed on two fronts, RAF Bomber Command could venture into making daylight raids over Germany. The Luftwaffe was short of fuel and trained pilots and was unable to make an effective defence of the Fatherland. British and American fighters with exceptional long-range capabilities could operate where and when they liked in the closing months of the most horrible and devastating war in human history.

On April 16th, 611 Squadron joined a Canadian Squadron to fly escort to 18 Lancaster bombers that were instructed to bomb Swinemunde in the Baltic.

Before the operation the fighter pilots received a warning. After bombers had turned for home the fighters were to head for Berlin and look for trouble. As the eastern front had swept closer to the German capital city, the pilots were told to watch out for Russian fighters. The Americans had experienced a brush with their Eastern allies and lost a number of Thunderbolts. Perhaps the Russians had mistaken the American fighters for FW190s.

Ron Mitchell had found himself wing-man to the Group Leader. He would be expected to stay with him should they hit trouble . . . As the Lancasters turned for home, the Mustang fighter escort turned south for Berlin. They had lost one of their charges but not to enemy fighters; it had been hit by AA fire. There was nothing that they could have done about that.

The Russian front lay below as they sped towards Berlin with the pilots peering around them.

"Fighters, ten o'clock low" came a cool, but urgent voice over the air.

Four . . . five . . . six, Ron counted. Four Yaks and two Shturmoviks. He could make out the red stars on the wings — what would happen if they were attacked? He didn't fancy the idea of getting into a scrap with the Ruskies! Nor did he fancy being involved in causing another war!

Group Leader Christie's voice came over the radios, "Let's get out of here — we don't want any trouble!"

As a man, the pilots of the Squadrons opened their throttles and left the Soviets standing.

The RAF and the Red Air Force had met up over the German capital and had not fought one another. Many in the German High Command had hoped that the Allies would fight it out — as East met West. Some entertained hopes of joining in a war against the Russians.

A few minutes after meeting the Russians, high over Berlin, 611's Adjutant Flying Officer Partridge called through, "Bandits — ten of 'em!"

"They'll be Ruskies!" replied the Group Leader. "Keep your eye on them."

Ron in the cockpit of his Mustang after the Berlin episode.

"They're Jerries . . . FW190's . . . " came the reply. "I can see the crosses!"

Ron Mitchell remained tucked in close to the Group Leader as the two Squadrons dived to the attack. He managed to get some shots in the direction of one of the German fighters but could not be sure of hitting it.

Soon, ten columns of smoke on the ground marked the outcome. Each of the German planes had been destroyed without losses to the Mustangs. The German pilots must have been made up of inexperienced youths, to have suffered such a defeat. This demonstrated the state that the German fighting forces had deteriorated to by the Spring of 1945.

After the war Ron continued to fly until Stand Down in January 1957, completing his career as a fighter pilot on the first jet fighters, Meteors and Vampires, with 614 Squadron.

He had flown practically every mark of Spitfire from the Battle of Britain type to the Griffon-engined later models. Then the Mustang long-distance fighters. He had "pranged" twice and on the second occasion, left a bit of his Spitfire on the Derbyshire hills.

Halifax HR952 of 51 Squadron is being prepared for a raid September, October 1943 IWM

Nightfighter Victim

Halifax HR727 of 51 Squadron returning to Snaith after bombing Frankfurt, crashed at Blackden Edge, October 5, 1943. Map reference 129879.

For each RAF aircraft crash in this country, a card was prepared outlining the briefest details. Form 1180, Accident Record Card, concerning the crash of Halifax HR 727 V for Victor, now held at the AHB (RAF) Ministry of Defence dated October 5th, 1943, contains the following information:

"Error in captaincy in breaking cloud when uncertain of position. Lack of fuel and faulty navigation. Pilot did not check Engineer's statement that there was four hours fuel left. Engineer failed to keep check and failed to warn of impending fuel shortage. Flight engineer chiefly responsible."

The above is the summary of an in depth inquiry instigated by the RAF Flight Safety organisation with the primary aim of avoiding similar accidents in the future. It was not possible to include a number of contributory factors to the accident, on Form 1180. As the full enquiry documents have since been destroyed, some possible factors are considered here.

The two survivors were Bomb Aimer Sergeant Victor Garland and Rear Gunner Sergeant Jimmy Mack. The conclusions drawn as to what contributed to the crash were gathered from statements taken from the injured men. Would either Garland or Mack find themselves in agreement with the official statements to be read on Form 1180?

Knowing what had happened on board V for Victor on that night in October 1943 could throw some light on the tragedy, some forty years after the event.

Sergeant Lane died shortly after the Halifax bomber hit the hilltop and consequently, his side of the story has never been told. With the help of the two survivors and an ex-Halifax flight engineer, the events have been reconstructed to put alongside the official Accident Record Card.

It was at 20 Operational Training Unit, Lossiemouth, that the crew came together. Each came from his individual training unit. There was the Pilot, Ernie Fenning, 21 years old and the only married man among them. Navigator was Canadian, 'Gil' Fortin, the grandfather of the crew who had reached the ripe old age of 25. Sergeant Victor Garland was the Bomb Aimer — from Aberdeen and a mere boy of 18. Wireless Operator — another teenager — Sergeant Frank Squibbs, and defending the rear, Sergeant Jimmy Mack aged 23, from Berwick-upon-Tweed.

At the OTU the crew learned to operate as a team flying Wellingtons — but they were incomplete, as a team of five. Later, at 1652 Heavy Conversion Unit, they took on the last two crew members, Mid-upper Gunner Sergeant Short (Shorty) and Engineer Eric Lane. The latest member was a necessary requirement for a crew moving onto four-engined bombers — Sergeant Lane was 21 years old. After completing their training, the new crew was ready to enter air battles over Europe and received a posting to 51 Squadron stationed at Snaith in Yorkshire.

The Squadron's unofficial name was "Yorks Own Squadron" and the previous year it had been engaged in anti-submarine patrols with Coastal Command; now equipped with Halifax II's however, it was back with Bomber Command in number 4 Group.

As the British bomber offensive grew in momentum towards the autumn of 1943, nightly excursions took in German cities further and further eastward towards Berlin; Mannheim, Kassel, Hanover and what some crews described as the "hottest" target — Frankfurt.

The first operation for the 'new boys' at 51 was a mine laying sorte on the 3rd September. Their first attack on a German city took place two nights later when around 500 bombers attacked Mannheim. A thousand acres of the city was devastated; four railway stations were gutted along with storehouses and sheds. Warehouses in the area around the river docks burned on for three days.

On the following night they made their longest flight over enemy territory when they visited Munich, the birth place of national socialism, they were nine and a half hours in the air. Short of fuel they landed at Hunsden, north of London, completing the journey back to Snaith next morning.

The men of V for Victor, of "Vicky" as they affectionately named Halifax HR 727, were beginning to knit together as a crew, gaining experience as they went on to other varied targets: Dunlop rubber factory at Montlucon; marshalling yards at Modane on the French Italian border; Hanover twice and Mannheim again. Bochum town centre was flattened at the end of September bringing Vicky's crew to the completion of their first month of operations.

On October 3rd they were among the 467 Main Force crews who attacked Kassel. Although the Germans had succeeded in decoying the British 'terror bombers' away from the city, one of the largest ammunition depots in Germany was inadvertantly hit. The resulting explosions attracted other aircraft and the dump was destroyed.

Losses to defending nightfighters in the last quarter of the year began to climb again as the Luftwaffe units began to receive new radar equipment to combat tinfoil jamming by the bombers.

In July — in an attack on Hamburg, strips of aluminium foil had been dropped in bundles by the raiders, blotting out the German radar screens. However, within a short two months, the scientists had come up with the "Lichtenstein SN-2" which once again gave the nightfighter crews the means to wreak havoc among the bomber streams. It was against this background that the events of the night of October 4th, 1943 took place.

Earlier that day Eric Lane had swung his legs out of bed and dragged on his uniform over his six foot frame. On his way to the ablutions, he checked the sky — would the weather hold? Would they be going that night? He made his way over to the station building and into the crew room to mark that he was present by placing a tick beside his name. The blackboard did not carry the message "stand down till" which would have meant an evening at the pub or the pictures — so he concluded that something would be on that night.

Borrowing a bike, he rode round the perimeter track to where the bombers were parked. It was his task to check the aircraft over and report back to the Skipper — Ernie Fenning — that everything was OK. A formality in a way, for the ground crews took real pride in their work and made sure that everything was spot on.

There she stood, £50,000's worth of heavy bomber — painted black on the sides and underneath the wings, the squadron identification letters MH at one side of the RAF roundel and the letter V on the other.

Eric dismounted and began his routine checks: cowlings, inspection covers etc., all in place and secure. No oil, fuel or hydraulic leaks, tyres and undercarriage legs OK, in fact, everything was in order — as he knew it would be. Hoisting himself through the hatch in the fuselage, Eric wandered down to the tail then back along the whole length of the aircraft, checking pressure gauges and pipes. Everything seemed to be in order — V for Victor was ready to go.

After lunch at the Mess, the tannoy announced "all crews to briefing at 1400 hours". The crews of each aircraft sat together in the Ops. Room facing a curtained-off map on the wall. There was a suspicion of a 'sticky' trip that night, some speculation was in the air concerning the type of bombs being loaded into their aircraft at that moment. Not mines, which would have indicated a reasonably easy trip to the Baltic to do some "gardening" but high explosives and incendiaries, meaning one of Hitler's cities . . . .

As the CO walked in, everyone sprang to attention. They were told to be seated and every eye was upon that man as he drew back the curtains, to reveal the large map of Europe. "Gentlemen," he announced. "Your target for tonight is Frankfurt." A thin, red ribbon dog-legged across the map into Germany, ending at the industrial town situated on the Main river. A groan went up from the assembled crews — it was going to be nasty.

The raid on Frankfurt on October 4/5th was to be a "maximum effort". In order to confuse the Germans and try to draw off the night-fighters, a 'spoof' raid was to be made on Ludwigshafen. In the event, this deceptive ploy was only partially successful.

Various bombing officers covered their own specialist subjects in turn; navigation, bombing, engineering, gunnery, meteorology and intelligence. Duration of the whole trip was estimated at around 8 hours. Fighter and anti-aircraft opposition was expected to be heavy. The target city would be marked with flares dropped by the Pathfinder Force.

The Met. Officer announced the far from cheery news that the then misty conditions would develop into a 'pea soup'. The Squadron would have to head north to clear it, pin point their position at Berwick-upon-Tweed before setting course for Germany. He went on to predict that the Base would be clear upon their return. His confident prediction was to be proved totally inaccurate as Britain began one of its worse nights of the year in regards to weather.

Each member of the crew of V for Victor absorbed all the particulars relevant to his own function — the briefing was over and it was time for the knots in the stomach, the pre-op. nerves and the tension. Casualties in

Rear gunner Jimmy Mack

Bomber Command were high and it had been calculated that over the years, around one in two would not survive.

What had come to be a tradition followed later that afternoon. The pre-operational meal of bacon and eggs. Then it was time for kitting up at the locker room where personal effects were handed over. The crew clambered into their flying gear and after collecting parachutes and testing microphones and headphones in their helmets, the crews climbed onto the trucks to be taken out to their respective aircraft.

Eric Lane gave the V for Victor another brief external check and had a word with the ground crew; he removed the pitot head cover and stuffed it in his battledress blouse. One by one each crew member slung his gear up through the hatch on the port side and jumped up after it.

All round the airfield at Snaith, wireless operators in their Halifax's switched on their sets to warm them up. Three hundred miles away in Belgium, German radio-monitoring stations picked up the radio signals and were alerted to a big raid threat — information was passed on to fighter operations rooms and nightfighters were put on standby. Once the final direction of the bomber stream had been determined, the individual twin-engined fighters would be vectored onto the raiders.

Eric Lane plugged in his intercom and awaited Skipper Ernie Fenning's orders to start up. When it came, it was a short trip back to the rest position (two couches mid-way between the main wing spars) to pull on the cocks for petrol tanks 1 and 3 in each wing. Back again to the engineer's panel situated in an area behind the "main office" or pilot's seat. At the Skipper's command, Eric Lane pressed the individual starter and booster buttons for each of the four Rolls-Royce Merlin engines. Each crew in turn reported to the pilot that their instruments and equipment were OK — it was time to move.

Ground staff guided the bomber from dispersal to the perimeter track where a queue was forming, awaiting takeoff.

From his position in the rear turret Jimmy Mack could see Halifax J for Jig moving up behind him and exchanged a wave with the bomb aimer, Sergeant Vose. As V for Victor was given the green light, he both felt and heard the concerted roar of all four engines as the Skipper opened the throttle and the following aircraft were quickly left behind as they surged down the runway. It was 5.30 and beginning to get dark, as the fog closed in.

It was always a tense moment as the heavily-loaded bomber passed the point of no return, just prior to it becoming "unstuck" from the ground. To lose an engine at that point would have meant ploughing on into the fields opposite — loaded with bombs and full tanks it was regarded by the crews as a dangerous exercise.

Once off the deck, the Flight Engineer's job was to make sure that the undercarriage was locked up and that the flaps isolating cock was off; then he would set the throttle and revs. for climbing.

Gilbert Fortin, the Canadian navigator, called through his instructions to the Skipper and V for Victor turned onto course to rendezvous with hundreds of other bombers including Lancasters and Halifaxes from other squadrons and groups over Berwick-upon-Tweed.

Every crew member settled down to his job with the Skipper checking with each one of them to see that everything was working.

Lying in his prone position in the nose, bomb aimer and teenager Victor Garland reported to the Navigator that they were crossing the English coastline.

Once out over the sea, the mid-upper gunner Sergeant Short and rear gunner Jimmy Mack requested and were given permission to test their machine guns.

"Navigator to pilot — turn to course 160°".

The other teenager W/Operator Frank Squibbs meanwhile had been listening out at various pre-arranged times for broadcasted revised wind changes. And for the dreaded message that the raid had been cancelled. This would have meant that all the effort and tension up to that point had been in vain — and that they would be unable to count that sorte against the required 30 operations which represented a tour. After each tour a crew could look forward to a six months rest from operational flying.

There was to be no recall from the Frankfurt raid.

Every twenty minutes Eric Lane entered the cylinder head temperatures on his log sheet along with oil pressures. Fuel consumption was his main concern, as he carefully worked out how much petrol was being used. He would switch from one tank to another — taking care not to let an engine cut through fuel starvation. The Halifax now sported six fuel tanks of various sizes in each wing; the Engineer had to juggle with thirteen levers or cocks to sort out the 1800 gallons or so. He had to bear in mind that takeoff, landing and over-target periods were critical and had to arrange things so at those times, he was on tanks 1 and 3 to the inner and outer engines respectively. This was because they were the largest and closest to the engines so consequently they were used at take off, over the target and landing. The rest of the tanks were used to fill the gaps. Easy, so long as nothing upset the system — such as losing one engine, or having a tank holed — then things could get very complicated for the Engineer.

"Enemy coastline ahead — keep your eyes peeled", came the Skipper's warning to all crew members.

All light banter on the intercom ceased now — it was to be used strictly for business from now on.

Their zig-zag path avoided flak concentrated areas of the heavily-defended Ruhr Valley, but they were now on the last leg leading up to the target. Ahead of the main bomber stream, Lancasters of the Pathfinder Force were busy putting down Blind Marker Illuminators which were falling within 3 miles of the aiming point. Greater accuracy was achieved when Primary Visual Markers dropped within $1\frac{1}{2}$ miles of the target centre.

At 9.10 V for Victor began its approach at 19,000 feet. Ahead of them the crew could see a mass of searchlight beams probing out into the sky, trying to latch on to one of the raiders. Bright orange and red bursts of flame ahead of them, indicating anti-aircraft shell explosions, seemed to warn against flying straight and level — but it was a necessary part of a bombing raid to run straight and steady up to the target. They had never seen so many searchlights.

"Navigator to Pilot — 15 minutes to target!"

The young Scot bomb aimer lying prone in the nose began busying himself setting wind, height, speed and the sequence in which the bombs were to be dropped, on his bombsight.

It was time for Eric Lane to move. Making his way back to the rest position he plugged in his intercom. "Engineer to Pilot" — "I'm changing to tanks 1 and 3, starboard, now!"

Pilot Fenning readied himself to throttle back any engine which might cut and to compensate for any resulting swing. The port engine switch followed with no trouble. Eric's next job was to whip out a screwdriver and remove the inspection covers above each bomb release mechanism. In the event of any bomb failing to drop, he would stick his finger through the hole and let it go manually. They were determined not to take any "hang ups" back with them!

"Pilot to Bomb Aimer, beginning the bomb run now . . . she's all yours . . ."

"Pilot to Gunners, watch out for fighters!"

The intercom was switched on permanently now and all members of the crew could hear young Vic Garland's voice as he relayed his instructions to Fenning.

"Keep her steady at that Skipper . . . left a bit . . . steady, steady, right, right, steady, now . . . steady . . ."

The young Scot's breathing between instructions could be heard plainly by each member of the crew as they sat tense in their positions. After what seemed an eternity the cross on the bomb sight moved onto one of the Pathfinder flares burning over 3 miles beneath them and the 18 year old youth pressed the button on the bomb release clenched in his right hand.

"Bombs gone!" he called.

All of them felt the gently upward swing as one 1000 pounder, one 500 pounder, 24 30 pounders and 540 4 pound incendiaries fell towards the city below. Through the open bomb doors, Eric Lane could see the inferno raging below.

"Engineer to Pilot, all bombs gone" he

Bomb aimer Vic Garland

reported. The bomb doors swung up and inwards as Fenning slammed up the bomb door lever. But the bomb run was not over yet.

"Pilot to Engineer — standby photo flash!"

A picture of the results was required and Eric moved over to the flare chute and despatched a most unwelcome passenger — a photo flare igniting in the centre fuselage could cause havoc. It meant flying straight and level, 30 seconds longer. The mid-upper gunner, Sergeant Short was the most relieved to see the photo flash dropped down the flare chute as he owned the behind that hung closest to it! They could now take evasive action should this be needed.

Meanwhile, the spoof raid on Ludwigshafen had not entirely fooled the enemy and the nightfighters had not been enticed there, probably because the marking was wide of target and the raid late in getting started. The main attack on Frankfurt was well underway which convinced the fighter controllers that it was the main target. This fact was obvious to the Messerschmitt 110 pilots

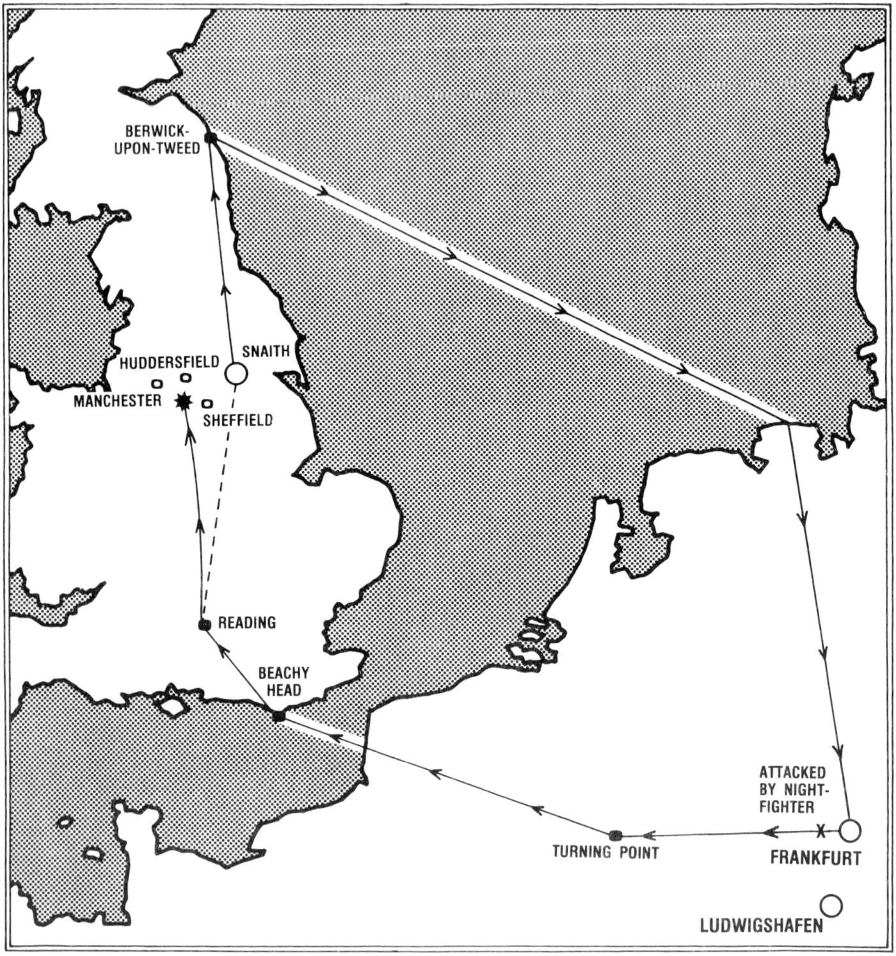

as they climbed to the height of the bombers. The fires burning at Frankfurt were plain enough to see.

"Navigator to Pilot, turn to course 280°".

They were going home. It was half-past nine, below and behind them, the city's railway marshalling yards, station buildings and warehouses were ablaze — a conflagration that was to last for 3 days.

In the rear turret crouched behind four Browning machine guns, Jimmy Mack avoided looking at the fires raging beneath in order not to destroy his night vision.

Suddenly, Jimmy Mack's turret turned into day — he was temporarily blinded as a searchlight beam struck V for Victor. Other beams immediately swung on to illuminate the bomber that had been caught and flak began bursting all around.

No need for any fancy stalking for the nightfighter that was closing in fast on V for Victor — the technique that they usually used was to pick up the bomber on their new Lichenstein SN-2 radar sets — close in beneath it and with twin upward pointing cannons, open fire at close range. The four-engined RAF bombers made excellent targets with their large wing areas packed with fuel tanks.

On this occasion, the searchlight batteries

had coned one of the hated enemy and the Messerschmitt pilot would take a chance on being hit by the concentrated flak barrage that was creeping across to the bomber.

Short, in the mid-upper turret glimpsed the closing nightfighter at the same time as 30mm cannon shells banged into the port inner engine.

"Fighter! Corkscrew port — GO!"

Ernie Fenning pushed the control column forward and slammed his left leg forward, at the same time opening the throttles. V for Victor powered down out of the searchlight's glare and under the attacking fighter with the port inner engine burning. Each crew member was pressed against the fuselage as Fenning swung the bomber violently to starboard midway through the dive. Their ears hurt as the pressure rapidly changed. They were doing around 300 mph as Fenning pulled into a climb and while still in the starboard turn, he pushed the nose down again going into a further dive.

It was a manoeuvre that was difficult for the most experienced fighter pilot to follow. After corkscrewing down to 9,000 feet they discovered that they had lost their attacker and that the engine fire was out. Fenning feathered the propeller on the dead engine and trimmed the aircraft for straight and level flight.

That little incident would play havoc with Eric Lane's calculations. His first job was to switch off port number 1 tank. Back at his panel he scanned the petrol gauges and fuel pressure warning lights for the 3 good engines. The needle on the gauge for number 2 tank started to creep back steadily. Eric Lane moved quickly back to the petrol cocks and plugged into the intercom.

"Engineer to Pilot, Number 2 tank holed with 64 gallons in — a third of our emergency reserve. Can I run all 3 engines from it to minimise losses?"

"Pilot to Engineer, go ahead — it's no use letting it go to waste." He readied himself to throttle back on any engine that should fail through fuel starvation.

With every move he made, Lane carried out a running commentary over the intercom.

"Turning off Number 3 . . . now! Turning on number 2, wing balance . . . open."

Suppose the pipes leading to the port outer engine had been fractured? Eric Lane had to take that possibility into account. He peered hard at the warning light to the port outer — not a flicker — it was OK.

"Port outer OK Skipper. Get ready for transfer to starboard!"

A locking wire trapped the transfer cock that would permit fuel to be transferred from one wing to the other. He kept up his vital commentary. If the Engineer got it right then there would be no fuel starvation to the two Merlins thundering away on the starboard wing.

"Cutting wire, Skipper. Main balance . . . on!"

He watched for a flicker on the starboard inner warning light — all was well. The delicate operation was completed without mishap. All three engines were pulling from the holed number 2 on the port wing. Unplugging his intercom, Lane moved back to his instrument panel and began checking each dial. He was relieved to note that the three engines were running sweet and were undamaged, and the other fuel tanks seemed sound. They had got off lightly — but he would have to concentrate on Number 2 gauge which was indicating around 55 gallons — the leak wasn't massive. All the crew reported that they were unhurt and that their instruments and equipment were working.

Eric Lane performed his next duty — taking a torch he checked through the aircraft for holes, sparks from damaged electrics and that reservoir pressures were normal. Again, he could report to the Skipper that everything was all right.

After 150 miles on the homeward trip, a further course change was made and the limping Halifax turned onto a north-westerly heading.

From his position in the tail, Jimmy Mack could see — even at that distance — the glow of fires as Frankfurt burned. Both he and the Upper Gunner, Short, were asked by the Skipper for an extra effort in keeping a look-out for nightfighters as they were well below the main bomber stream and alone.

Back in the Engineer position, Eric Lane began his calculations. These were vital for their safe return to Snaith. He dare not let the damaged Number 2 tank fall below 20 gallons and run the risk of 3 engines cutting out altogether. He totalled up the fuel in the good tanks then read off the engine revs. boost and altitude. From this he worked out the fuel consumption, divided one from the other and the figure he was left with was the flying time.

"Engineer to Pilot, 4 hours flying time left."

The Canadian Navigator, Gilbert Fortin, using the Engineer's figures, was able to give an estimated time of arrival — at around 1.15 they would be home — that was if the winds didn't change . . .

"Pilot to Engineer, can you give me a rundown on what accessories we have lost?"

That was another problem for Eric Lane to consider. Each of the four engines drove generators and pumps which performed various functions throughout the aircraft — lose an engine and you lost certain services. Eric Lane began a list of services that they would be unable to call upon because of the port inner engine having stopped turning. Wheel brakes, automatic pilot, undercarriage flaps, radiator shutters . . . Certain vital functions they would have to operate manually by emergency means. Electrically, the generator on the port inner packed juice into a 24 volt accumulator which in turn, provided power for the mid-upper turret and — most vital of all — the beam approach equipment and radio.

With Number 2 gauge indicating 20 gallons left, Eric Lane began to juggle the petrol cocks to get back to the comparative safety of one tank, one engine. There was equal fuel in each wing, but the starboard side was being used at twice the rate, so unless he could balance the position they would end up with empty tanks on one side — and a heavy load on the other — with only one engine to bear it. Both he and the Skipper were confident that they could cope with this problem.

V for Victor crossed the enemy coast and was soon over the Channel.

"Bomb Aimer to Navigator, we are over Beachy Head!"

They were on course and heading for their beds in Yorkshire — another op. under their belts.

The bomber with its dead engine droned on northwards towards a heavy weather front that was moving across central and northern England. "Wireless Operator to Pilot. Bad reception Skipper — can't pick up met. report."

Young Squibbs, the 18 year old, "Sparks" was operating a steadily dying set as power in the accumulator was being used up. With the help of the Navigator he let out a trailing aerial to try and improve reception. With the bad weather and the fuel situation, this was no time for the aircraft to go deaf with radio failure. They needed those weather reports — every half-hour.

"Bomb Aimer to Navigator — we are over Reading!"

As the bomber entered the bad weather front, the wireless gave up. No more help for the navigator, no radio direction finding aid, no broadcast revised winds, no emergency calls on "Darkie" to anyone on the ground. They were deaf

They were also blind — they could see no landmarks as rain lashed the limping aircraft.

"Navigator to Pilot — we are port of track Skipper — that's if the winds haven't changed. We should be over base in 15 minutes."

The Skipper, Ernie Fenning, had to make some decisions and make them fast. He knew that he could not hang around in the clouds. Fuel situation was critical and he would need time over the drome to determine the serviceability of the undercarriage. If it had been damaged by the nightfighter's attack, then they would have to divert to a grass emergency landing strip and time was rapidly running out. A decision had to be made fast. The altimeter was showing around 2,000 feet and they were still in cloud. If they could get below it they might "pundit" crawl the remaining distance. That was, using the marker beacons flashed by each individual airfield along their flight track they would arrive safely. They had successfully used this method in the past.

Vic Garland, the bomb aimer, left his position in the nose and stood in the second pilot's position, ready to give his Skipper some help pointing out any flashing light beacon that they might spot as they broke cloud.

"Engineer to pilot — we're almost out of fuel Skipper." Eric Lane expected at any moment his three faithful Merlins would splutter to a stop.

"Pilot to Crew — watch your ears — I'm going down . . . "

V for Victor never went into that descent. Vic Garland recalled what happened next:

"Suddenly, I felt that I was in a small room about five feet wide — getting thrown from one wall to the other. When I came to, I was lying with parts of the cockpit surrounding me. I tried to stand, but found that my ankles were broken . . . "

In the rear turret, Jimmy Mack thought that they must have struck another aircraft. He remembers being banged about in his small confined space, ending up lying on the moorland. As he lay there, looking up into the swirling blackness of the night, it all seemed ominously quiet and strange. Having had the vibration and roar of Merlin engines for the past eight hours, it was suddenly quite peaceful in a way.

Jimmy's limbs all seemed to be in order and he was able to stand, but where was the remainder of the aircraft? He could make out his turret and some tail section, but the rest of the aircraft, fragmented and broken, spilled off into the darkness.

K. A. MERRICK

Halifax HR727 had been used for rudder experiments before going to 51 Squadron. Jimmy Mack's 'office' from which he escaped with his life can be clearly seen.

The sound of a whistle broke the silence. Someone was alive out there in the darkness of the moorland. Jimmy Mack took his own whistle which was attached to his battle dress blouse collar and gave an answering blast. Following the sound of the whistle, Jimmy eventually traced Eric Lane.

"I'm hurt bad Jimmy," Eric gasped. He appeared to be in a great deal of pain but Jimmy could find no marks upon him.

Fifteen feet further on, lying amidst the shattered wreckage of the cockpit, Jimmy Mack stumbled on Vic Garland.

"It's my ankles — they're in a mess but I think I'm not too bad — check on the others."

Nearby, Skipper Ernie Fenning lay — he had died instantly. Hunting around the wreckage Jimmy came upon Fortin, Short and the young teenage wireless operator Frank Squibbs. All three were dead.

"I'm going for help" Jimmy informed the other two survivors, as he made them as comfortable as he could.

"Don't leave me Jimmy," groaned the Engineer. "I'm dying . . . "

A curved sheet of armour plate.
Opposite: girders and metal sheeting litter the site.

"You'll be all right Eric — Vic Garland is in a worse state than you. There's not a mark on you . . . " So saying, the rear gunner began his descent off Blackden Edge, in Derbyshire, where the shattered Halifax had so suddenly and tragically come to rest.

They were a few minutes flying time from home — but with no flying aids, high ground and the appalling weather conditions, it had made little difference to the ill-fated crew of V for Victor.

The crash had taken place between 1 and 1.30 a.m. and it was around noon on the following afternoon when the site was located by the rescue services. Eric Lane had died during that time — his injuries were of a massive, internal kind. Garland and Jimmy Mack were taken to Sheffield Infirmary then transferred to an RAF hospital. After four months Vic Garland was then transferred to an aircrew convalescent home at Hoylake in Cheshire and after three months there he was posted as an Instructor to a conversion unit. From there, Vic Garland joined another aircrew and flew a further 26 bomber operations with 51 Squadron. The injuries to both his ankles did not prevent him from playing for Scotland at lawn tennis and table tennis. He is now a senior technical representative with a large paper mill.

Jimmy Mack joined another crew pending a medical to see whether he was fit for flying on 'Ops.' He was taken off on medical grounds. On the very first operation, the crew that he had been assigned to, failed to return. Now he serves as butler and valet to Sir Ralph Carr-Ellison, T.D., D.L., Hedgeley Hall, Northumberland.

Who was responsible for the crash of V for Victor? The Accident Record Card at the Ministry of Defence (which is a summary of the in depth proceedings of an enquiry) states — "Flight engineer chiefly responsible". There is no room to mention the loss of one engine and the resulting loss of other essential functions. No mention of the appalling weather conditions on the approaches to Snaith — stress and fatigue are not recorded on Form 1180. Where did the responsibility lie for the crash of Halifax HR 727?

Consider for a moment: teenagers and young men — barely in their twenties, formed into teams and given charge of complex flying machines after a basic minimum of training. Sent off in the night on round trips upwards of 1,000 miles to unload deadly explosives and incendiary devices on German citizens. Eight hours in the air — hounded by searchlights, anti-aircraft fire and hunting, marauding

nightfighters — in danger from mid-air collisions with other bombers and with bombs dropping from aircraft flying above them. Dogged by equipment failures and atrocious weather conditions. These were all factors which had to be handled about twice or three times a week. This went on, month after month until chance and cold statistics caught up with a crew and scrubbed them from the active service list — placing them on memorial rolls.

Who was responsible for the crash? If not man's insistance on going to war, then blame could be laid with the nightfighter pilot who wrote off V for Victor's port inner engine over Frankfurt.

A large sheet of armour and an inspection cover bearing the markings "OIL X/X".

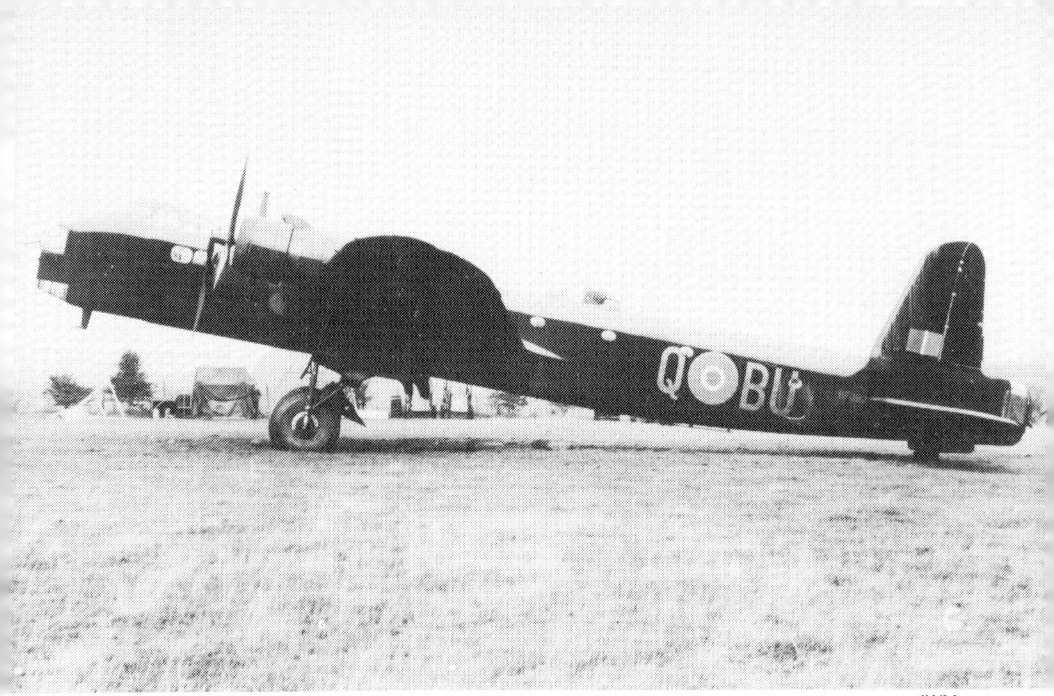

IWM

First And Last Time

Stirling LJ 628 of 1654 Heavy Conversion Unit, Wigsley, practising two and three engine flying, crashed on Upper Commons, July 21, 1944. Map reference 198954.

It was a far cry from the "Wimpy's" that they had been trained on at 29 Operational Training Unit, Sergeant Coulson decided as he gazed up at the Stirling bomber towering above him.

He had been selected and trained as a bomb aimer and had become part of a crew at 29 OTU Bruntingthorpe near Lutterworth in Leicestershire. For the final part of their training, they had been posted to 1654 Heavy conversion Unit at Wigsley and Swinderby near Lincoln.

It was July 1944, the invasion of Europe had taken place the previous month and the RAF Bomber offensive was at it's peak. Losses were heavy among bombers and the HCU's were busy supplying replacement crews. Each month, 30 to 35 new crews were being passed out on four-engined aircraft from each of the HCU's.

Mainstay of the conversion units was the Short Stirling. First of the RAF heavy four-engined bombers, the Stirling had been gradually relegated to training roles because of operational shortcomings.

The wings were short, Jim Coulson observed, making the fuselage seem disproportionately long.

Not the fault of the designer at Short Brothers, who had faithfully created the Stirling to an Air Ministry specification. Standard RAF aircraft hanger doors were 100 feet wide so it had been carefully specified that the four-engined bomber should have a wing span less than this. With that restriction, the resultant aircraft was unable to fly at any great height.

As enemy defensive ground fire improved, the Stirling became an easy target as it came in over the area to be bombed at a mere 12,000 feet. The designers had been forced by the laws of aerodynamics, to place their short length wings mid-way up the fuselage. This in turn meant an enormous ungainly undercarriage holding the Stirling at an angle that would ensure sufficient lift to get it airborne.

Jim Coulson was six feet tall and yet he could barely peer over the wheels of the mighty giant aircraft. It would be the Skipper's job to learn to handle the Bristol Hercules four engines in the next few weeks, but to the young Londoner, it seemed that

Bomb aimer Jim Coulson

their pilot would be hard put just taking off and landing the Stirling.

F/O Gardiner had again looked through the pilot's notes on the Stirling, prior to his crews' first training flight that morning. Under the section headed "take off" he had noted a cautionary warning: "Open the throttles slowly (holding all four levers with one hand) the starboard throttles leading, to counteract the slight tendency to swing to starboard."

As pilot and skipper he had been warned that the Stirling tended, on take off, to veer to the right and numerous accidents had occurred as heavily-laden bombers had swung off the runway at speed and gone careering across the airfield. Apparently, this tendency was far from slight for all novice pilots. It was to be a full aircraft that morning for the crew's first flight. There were the six original crew members who had come together at 29 OTU. Pilot F/O Gardiner; Navigator Sergeant McDonald from Inverness; Bomb-aimer Sergeant Jim Coulson and Wireless Operator Sergeant "Tex" Burroughs — both from London; Rear gunner Sergeant "Swig" van Nierkirk and Mid-upper gunner Sergeant "Bunny" Austin, both Rhodesians.

With conversion to four engines, a flight engineer had joined the crew and he was along for the first time. Showing him the 'ropes' was Flight Engineer, Sergeant John Gittings, who was 'resting' after doing a tour of operations with 467 Squadron.

Sitting in the second pilot's seat as flying instructor was F/O O'Leary. Quite a crowd — but then, to top it all, a Squadron Leader elected to fly with them. Ten men in total in Stirling Mark III, LJ 628.

A constant flow of intercom chatter between pilot and engineer preceded take off. Jim Coulson as bomb aimer took no part in this — he was along for the ride. He had moved back from the nose, which seemed a heck of a long way from the ground — ready for take off.

Under the watchful eye of pilot instructor O'Leary, Gardiner opened the throttle gradually until all four engines were running at 2000 rpm. He then released the brakes and the bomber began to move forward.

The expected swing to the starboard came early, but he was ready for it and easing the control column forward as they gathered speed, Gardiner caused the huge tail to lift. They were doing around 110 mph as they eased off the ground.

Once the enormous undercarriage had been retracted, Jim Coulson moved back into the nose and began to familiarise himself with the layout. At least he had more room here than he had lying prone, in the nose of the Wellington.

It was 10.05 as Stirling LJ 628 lifted from the runway at Wigsley and climbed above the clouds.

Once they had reached 10,000 feet, Gardiner was given the feel of flying a four-engined bomber, first with one engine stopped — then another. They knew that they were over the flat countryside of Lincolnshire and began to execute a rated descent into the cloud cover with one engine stopped. They had been flying for about 20 minutes.

In the nose, Jim Coulson busied himself checking for leaks. He swung himself up into the front turret and began an examination in there. Cloud swirled about the perspex as he took his "little black book" and started to make an entry. He glanced up, could hardly believe his eyes, and yelled into the intercom;

"Pull up the flaming nose Skipper!"

The ground was rushing rapidly up to meet them!

The reaction by Gardiner was immediate — he pulled hard on the control column and the Stirling reared up and "bellied on" the moorland. They were 45 miles east of where they thought they were.

The initial impact bounced the rear turret off the plane — complete — with "Swig" van Nierkirk still in it. Tail and wings were ripped off as the giant bomber bumped and slewed across Upper Commons, Bradfield, near Sheffield.

Three escape hatches along the fuselage were thrown open and six men scrambled out bruised and shaken. The two flight engineers were able to scramble out through the open end of the broken fuselage.

The Squadron Leader took one quick check — two missing: Coulson and Nierkirk. One look at the smashed and squashed Bomb aimer's position and they feared the worst for Jim.

Then a groaning was heard coming from the crumpled nose — Jim Coulson was alive.

Access to the nose was cut off from inside the aircraft in the cockpit. An axe stowed behind the pilot's seat was brought out and the ones least shaken were ordered to cut the bomb aimer out. There was little fire risk as the wings containing the fuel tanks had been ripped away from the fuselage.

Jim Coulson was lifted through the jagged opening, laid gently on the ground on a opened parachute while the others bandaged his injured leg and head.

Flight Engineer, instructor, Sergeant John Gittings recalls the events of that morning:

"I was standing up looking out of the astrodome facing the rear of the aircraft. The cloud was very dense but I think that I did glimpse a lake below through an odd break in the cloud.

"We started to descend through the cloud, one minute we were flying, the next I was flung six to eight feet up the fuselage and ended up sprawled across the other flight engineer. The aircraft was slithering along the ground.

"Once we came to a stop the flight engineer expressed concern for the rear gunner. We made our way to the rear of the aircraft only to find that the fuselage had broken in two. We ran out onto the moor and up to the tail section — the rear turret was missing. Immediately we set off up the moor to find it and eventually located it, only to find it empty. In the meantime some of the others had located the rear gunner, Swig Van Nierkirk, lying under the broken tail. We had run right past him.

Flight engineer John Gittings

"No one had any idea where we were. Two of the crew were given a compass and sent off to get help. As no help had arrived by 2 p.m. Squadron Leader Hadland and another crew member set off to try and find out where we were.

"Six hours after we had crashed help arrived in the shape of the Chief Flying Instructor from Wigsley, Squadron Leader Petty and two army chaps carrying stretchers, guided by two members of the crew.

"We all left the aircraft and walked taking it in turns to carry the injured. After about an hour we reached the road and from there the wounded were taken to hospital. The rest of us stayed at an army camp for the night.

"Next morning we were picked up by lorry and taken back to Wigsley, calling on the way at a Sheffield Hospital to see how Coulson and Van Nierkirk were."

The two injured men were taken to Wharncliffe Hospital by members of an RAMC Unit, where they both underwent operations.

First to recover was the Rhodesian Rear Gunner, "Swig" who was able to rejoin the crew — and along with them was posted to 44 Squadron where they completed a tour of operations — and survived the war.

After six weeks, Jim Coulson went to Lancaster Finishing School at Syerston and to a new crew. He was welcomed at the LFS by his new Skipper — a Canadian-Chinese named F/O A. E. Jung. With this new crew, Jim completed a tour with 50 Squadron, flying in Lancasters. He never again set foot in a Stirling bomber — his trip on that fateful morning of July 21st, 1944 had been his first and last flight in that historic aircraft type.

He went to live in Canada in 1951 with his wife Anne, an ex-photographer in the WAAF. Jim Coulson died on March 25th, 1979.

Ex-crew member of Stirling LJ628, John Gittings returned to the scene of the crash in September 1981. Here he stands among the wreckage (centre) pointing out how the heavy bomber ended up to two of his guides to the site, Mr. Gerald Scarret and Mr. Norman Winterbottom.

"Tex" Burroughs, who now lives in New Zealand and works as a Avionic's Instructor with Air New Zealand, remembers the events surrounding the accident and tells the story in his own words.

"I don't know any of the details that led up to the crash, because I was on Radio the majority of the time, only coming back on the crew intercom to report weather reports or the results of check broadcasts.

What is still very clear in my mind is looking out of my window and thinking how close the ground had now become. Before I could make any comment on this to the Captain or pass on any weather info, we had hit!

I remember bracing myself with my hands pressed against my work desk and pushing back into my very efficient and well-upholstered chair. This was a first class piece of furniture — and I'm sure it helped in a big way to protect me from injury. There next followed an awful screeching and screaming of heavily tortured meal — associated with

Mr. Gittings here posing by one of the Stirling's wheels which is still complete with tyre and inner tube. The other undercarriage unit lies buried close by.

Wireless operator Tex Burroughs

lots of ups and down, until one violent movement sent me sideways out of the seat, to crash into the electrical panel.

I slithered down this and sat in a somewhat dazed heap on the floor. Someone shouted a warning, the full text of which I have forgotten; but I do remember it contained the word "Fire"!

In the next instant I was up and out of that aircraft so fast! In retrospect, this is where my training came to the fore. Because to this day I cannot remember having to duck under the oxygen bottles which were arranged in a circular arrangement over the main spar — or for that matter, having to negotiate the main spar in my dash to evacuate by the rear door. I just went straight down the fuselage and out — but in this case not by the rear door — instead, through the gap left by the now departed rear turret. This, we found several yards back from where the aircraft came to rest. The rear gunner — a young lad called Lennox VanNiekerk, was knocked out cold. Van Niekerk was from Que-que in Rhodesia.

The Bomb Aimer was retrieved from amongst the heather and mud and what remained of the Bomb Aimer's compartment in the nose section, he apparently having been there at the time, looking — so I heard — for a landmark!

His name was James Coulson and he came from Hackney, London. He never caught up with the crew again after this. Both these boys were covered with parachutes to keep them warm, given first aid and placed under what remained of the port wing. A further 'chute was rigged to keep the cold out and we tried to make them as comfortable as possible.

Two of the crew, I believe, my Captain, Flight Lieutenant Gardiner and the Commander of 'B' Flight a Squadron Leader whose name I can't recall, took off across the moors to get help. In the meantime, in addition to keeping up the spirits of the injured, I tried my radio and found that the receiver still worked! In spite of my efforts though, I could not get the transmitter to function.

I then thought of the Dinghy Radio — here was a chance for me to try it out for real — so out it came — up went the kite (there was plenty of wind) and then I spent some time grinding away at the handle, sending out an automatic distress signal.

Whether anyone received this and what action was taken if they had, I never did find out. Its range would have been pretty limited in that area I think, but whoever it was who encouraged me in my efforts must have thought that this would at least keep me busy.

After what appeared to have been some considerable lapse of time, help arrived in the form of uniformed men with a couple of stretchers. We placed the injured crew members on these and trekked off across the moorland in the direction from which the help had come. Carrying those guys over the ups and downs across the gulleys, through the heather and the gorse to the transport, seemed endless. If someone now said it was "X" miles you covered, I would not argue! It sure seemed like a long way.

I remember going with the two injured in an ambulance to a Wharncliffe Emergency Hospital outside Sheffield — I can recall arriving there very well because there was a queue of them waiting outside to disgorge their wounded. For I was told that the battle for Caen in France was at its height! We had a little wait before we could get unloaded, and looked after. I was given a bed for the night and found myself next to some poor soldier boy who had copped a packet from a phosphorus bomb — nevertheless he was so cheerful in spite of looking like the invisible man in all his bandages. He must have been in great pain, too.

A funny thing happened to me whilst there. I had been to have a bath and was on my way back to the ward when I took a wrong turn, finishing up in a ward chock-a-block with Jerry wounded. So here I was confronted with the enemy. Face to face for the first time! It was a very strange feeling and I did a quick recovery — a sharp 180° turn and got out quickly. The rest of the crew so I was told, spent the night being entertained in some Army Rest Camp. I don't recall how we made it back to camp or what transpired when we did.

I know the "WOPs" were pleased to see me alive. I remember being sent on survival leave and how pleased my family was — also to know I was still alive and kicking, because they had received a telegram saying that I had been in an aircraft crash but that was all.

Things are pretty vague after that — I cannot recall if there was an investigation and if there was if I was involved. The crew, with the exception of the Bomb Aimer, stayed together and completed a tour on Lancasters with 44 Rhodesian Squadron.

Gully containing the remains of one wing.

Avro Anson

"AEROPLANE"

One of Sikorski's Tourists

Anson N9853 of 16 Service Flying Training School, Newton, flying to Millom, crashed on Edale Moor, December 11, 1944. Map reference 101878.

It was with reference to the sizeable contingent of Polish army and airforce personnel that found their way to the west that Hitler formed the nickname of "Sikorski's Tourists."

Defeated in the invasion of their country by the Germans in the west and the Russians in the east, thousands of Poles following devious routes, reached French soil to continue the fight. With the collapse of France, once again the Poles as units and as individuals, departed — this time for Britain where they became an effective force in the war effort of the Allies.

Each Pole who made the journey to the British Isles has a story to tell of his personal experiences of escape and his fight against Nazi Germany.

On December 11th, 1944 an Avro-Anson carrying five of Sikorski's Tourists crashed at Edale, injuring two of them.

One of the injured was Jan Klimczak. He was the station's electrical engineer at 16 Service Flying Training School at Newton in Nottinghamshire. The purpose of the trip that morning was to take three pilot instructors to Millom in Cumbria. Flying Officer Jan Klimczak was going along to inspect some new American electrical and navigational equipment. Operating the wireless was Flight Sergeant Pasinski.

Adverse weather conditions had restricted flying during the first few days of December, but conditions had improved on the morning of the 11th.

By 9.30 they were airborne and heading north. Klimczak was at the front beside the pilot. None of them bothered to strap themselves in — after all, it was just a routine flight — a 130 miles trip. As they approached the Pennines, the clouds closed in and snow swirled about the old "station bus" as the Anson was affectionately known.

The pilot, Chelstowski, decided to drop through the clouds to check his position. It appeared a safe enough manoeuvre as the altimeter was showing a healthy 2,500 feet.

Jan Klimczak peered up at what seemed to be a cockpit light and wondered who had put it there. He made a mental note to rebuke someone for carelessness when he got back — it was a stupid place to instal a light. Someone was crying out in pain. That noise seemed to have taken the place of the roar of the twin Cheetah engines. He would go to sleep again . . .

What Klimczak did not realise was that they were no longer in the air. Shortly before 10.00, Anson N9853 had descended through cloud and slammed into Edale Moor. The aircraft lay on its back — the light that the dazed electrical engineer had seen in the "roof" was in fact, a hole in the floor.

He had been rolled into a ball by the impact, breaking both arms and a leg. The pilot Chelstowski, was being pulled through the windscreen when Klimczak again regained consciousness. Two of the passengers, Flight Lieutenant Mecinski and Flight Lieutenant Suida, had escaped serious injury and were able to minister to the others.

An attempt was made to extract Klimczak from the wreckage, through the side of the broken fuselage, but it was too difficult a job — it would take axes to cut him free. Parachutes were opended by Mecinski and Suida and they wrapped them around their injured comrades.

It was Mecinski who went for help — walking down from Upper Tor towards Edale. At around 2 p.m. that day, a rescue party from the village arrived on the scene and firemen cut free Klimczak from the wreckage.

The wireless operator, Pasinski, was in a great deal of pain as he had suffered injuries

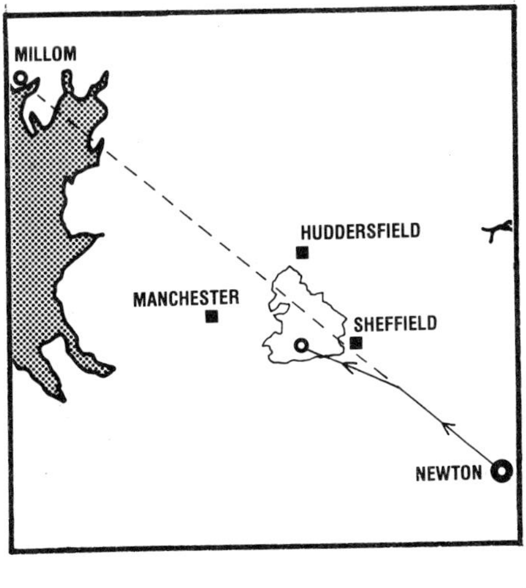

Jan Klimczak

Witold Suida

to his liver. He and Klimczak were the most seriously injured. From the crash site, they were taken to the hospital at RAF Wilmslow, where Klimczak lay unconscious for eleven days. There was a big gap in his right leg which required four inches of hip bone grafting in.

After 22 months of recuperation, he posted to 3 FTS at Feltwell for electrical duties.

Because of the shortage of electrical engineers, Klimczak — despite his injuries — served for a further two years. He was granted an 80 per cent disablement retirement from the RAF and settled in Collingham near Newark, with his wife — whom he had met whilst serving at Newton. He opened an electrical business from which he has recently retired.

All six Polish airmen, who were involved inthe crash at Edale, survived the war. The pilot, Flight/Lieutenant Chelstowski, received the blame for the accident. It was considered by the investigating officers that there had been negligence on his part and his pilot's log book was endorsed "gross carelessness".

Jan Klimczak, however, blames not the pilot but rather the altimeter, which was an old Mk 1 type and permitted a 500 feet errror. That amount of error margin was unacceptable when flying through clouds stuffed with hills . . . a regular feature of the Peak District.

One of the two Cheetah engines at the crash site receiving a thorough examination by some 'experts'.

It wasn't the first time that one of Sikorski's Tourists had been involved in an aeroplane crash and ended upside down. When he was twenty-one years old, as a reservist serving at a place called Puck on the Baltic Coast, Jan Klimczak had been ordered by the station's commanding officer to go along as "ballast". The CO was determined to get some flying hours. The aircraft was a two seater bi-plane, a French Potez 25. As they were coming in to land, on the short length field, the tailplane struck a high banking and the aircraft landed upside down. They hung from their seat straps with aviation fuel soaking them from the ruptured tank. Klimczak was able to free himself and rescue his CO who was caught up and terrified of being burned alive should the fuel ignite.

On that occasion there were no injuries. Nine years later, Jan Klimczak was to flee his homeland never to return . . .

Within a few weeks of the invasion of Poland by the Germans, the young Polish electrical engineer was to begin a 5000 mile trip, starting from a secret airfield at Wielicko in eastern Poland and ending in Liverpool, England.

Early in the morning of September 1st 1939, on two sections of the 1750 miles frontier with Poland, the Germans launched their attack.

At great speed the German mechanised

Wooden sections and metal fragments litter a gully on Edale Moor.

columns overtook Polish Army units which were falling back to man rearward positions. The army was being divided into unco-ordinated units by the enveloping actions of the Panzer divisions.

On September 3rd, Britain and France declared war on Germany.

Jan Klimczak was on his annual holiday in August 1939. He returned home at the end of the month to find himself a wanted man! The police had been searching for him since August 21st with his mobilisation papers. (He was a reservist). That day he reported to his unit, the 27th Technical Unit of the First Air Regiment, in Warsaw — stationed temporarily on the racecourse.

By now, military units, where they could, were moving east, hoping to re-group. On 2nd September, 27th Technical Unit moved all their equipment to the marshalling yards of Warsaw Central Station. Loaded on cattle waggons, they too moved east — a slow journey, the lines being crammed with military traffic and refugees. That night they reached Kowel, and from there continued by motor transport to a secret air base twenty miles south of the town.

As he surveyed the huge estate, there was nothing to indicate the presence of bomber aircraft — no runways, just open, flat fields skirted by woods. Beneath the trees were twin engined PZL P37 Los bombers. It was a small, fast aircraft — yet able to carry 5688lbs of bombs. The Polish airforce did not possess enough of these to hinder seriously the invasion — but at that point, Jan Klimczak was not to know that fact.

There were no tents and that night he slept under the stars with the 105 men of his unit.

In the days that followed the airfield was prepared for operations. Fuel was brought up by horse-drawn wagons and buses were commandeered to transport bombs to the field.

With the Polish Field Forces cut off by the pincer movements of the enemy, the Polish Commander-in-Chief, Marshall Rydz-Smigly, ordered a general retreat into the south-east of Poland. A week later operations ceased at the secret airfield and 27th Technical Unit was ordered to drive for the Romanian border.

Thirty lorries with equipment and portable workshops moved out from Wielicko and during that journey the convoy was attacked on three occasions by German aircraft, as they pushed on day and night through the

A Polish airfield prior to the German and Soviet invasion. In the foreground are the ground crew and crew of a PZL P37 LOSB bomber. In the background are obsolete Polish fighter PZL P11C's.

streams of refugees and miscellaneous military units.

On September 17th, the forces of the Soviet Union advanced from the east. This was signalled to the personnel of the 27th Technical Unit when an aircraft flew over sporting the red star of the Soviet Air Force. They knew then that all was lost.

The column turned away from before the red invasion and headed for Hungary. With Russsian tanks just five miles away, they crossed the border at Jasenie. With the column still in complete order, the 27th drove into Monkachevo where they handed over their arms and equipment to the Hungarian authorities. According to international law, they were interned here. The camp where they were held was a chicory factory at Nagy-Kanizsa, 125 miles from the capital city of Budapest.

They would have to escape, Jan Klimczak decided. As they had passed through the railway station at Budapest, a woman had slipped a card with and address upon it to one of the men from the unit.

One of the internees was a postman; his clothes would not, it was decided, create as much attention as those of a Polish airman. An exchange was arranged and the postman got the best of the deal. He had escaped the German invasion by walking from Poland to Hungary, his shoes were worn out and his suit was in tatters. Two others managed to change their uniforms for civilian clothes and joined Klimczak.

They broke out of the internment camp and caught a train to Budapest — arriving at the address they had been given on the slip of card, late at night. Fearing some sort of trap, the three Poles hid in the bushes and watched the house for a time. Eventually, a car drew up outside and the mystery woman emerged with some others — including a Hungarian Officer in uniform.

The three escapees could hear the group talking — in Polish — and it was this that made them decide to take a chance. They approached the group and produced the slip of card. The Hungarian officer, at this point, discreetly disappeared. Mr. Klimczak comments:

"Their flat was already filled with fleeing Poles — so we stayed the night with the chauffeur. Next day, the woman fitted me up with one of her husband's suits; it was of good quality, for her husband was a professor at Budapest University."

The next day, they were taken to the Polish Consulate where they easily avoided the guard which the Hungarians had placed on the door. Once inside the building they were issued with passports and money — visas were stamped on the passports that would take them to England.

'Tourists' on the run arrive in Athens, Klimczak is on the right in his borrowed suit.

They were directed to a train that would take them to Belgrade in Yugoslavia, where once again, at the Polish Consulate there, they were given money and train tickets — this time for Athens.

An efficient system seemed to have been established, processing escaping Polish military personnel through south-eastern Europe across the Mediterranean to France, where they could be re-formed to take up the fight once more.

In Athens, Jan Klimczak and his fellow-travellers joined a group of around fifty Polish airmen and, in a Greek ship, set sail for France. On October 16th 1939, they landed at Marseilles. A French Air Force officer met them and sent the group on to Brittany to a camp near Rennes, where, as a Polish unit, they served along with the French Air Force on various stations.

In the following year in the month of May, the mighty German war machine rolled westward and once again Klimczak was on the move. After the fall of Dunkirk, he — along with thousands of others — moved south-west through France towards Spain.

At the French port of St. Jean de Luz, a liner, the "Arandora Star" was being hastily

A motley crew of Poles arrived in France and formed into units of the French Air-Force. Klimczak is in the first row standing, seventh from the left.

Resplendent in French Air-Force uniforms Klimczak and two fellow 'tourists' make friends with the mademoiselles.

laden — she was bound for England. Two attacks by German aircraft underlined the extreme urgency of the situation and the need for rapid departure. Polish Air Force personnel were being granted priority places in the queue to board the liner, so Jan Klimczak found himself on deck when the liner sailed out into the Bay of Biscay on June 25th 1940.

On the four day trip to Liverpool, they were surprised to learn over the radio that the Arandora Star had been sunk with 8,000 Polish Air Force men on board! They landed safely at Liverpool and for Klimczak, it was the end of a 5000 mile trip.

For a time he served with 305 (Polish) Squadron which operated Wellingtons, as a ground electrical engineer. Then he moved to 16 Service Flying Training School at Newton, where he survived the crash on the moors above Edale.

Hitler's name for the Polish fighting men who had escaped when their country was ruthlessly crushed by the enemy, only to continue the struggle under the leadership of General Sikorski, was an apt name. And it was a name that Jan Klimczak would not dispute. He is proud to have been one of "Sikorski's Tourists."

Above: The tour continues as 8,000 members of the Polish Air Force sail, from France aboard the 'Arandora Star'.

Left: Another nation, another uniform — Jan looks slightly bewildered in his RAF gear.

Right: General Sikorski commander of his touring countrymen.

Below: 305 (Polish) Squadron Personnel firmly established as an important part of RAF Bomber Command.

Above: King George 6 inspects the newly formed Polish units. General Sikorski is on the King's right.
Below: Jan Klimczak after the crash at Edale which left him with a heavy scar on his right cheek.

Mr. Klimczak in 1981 with some of the 'souvenirs' he collected as one of Sikorski's tourists.

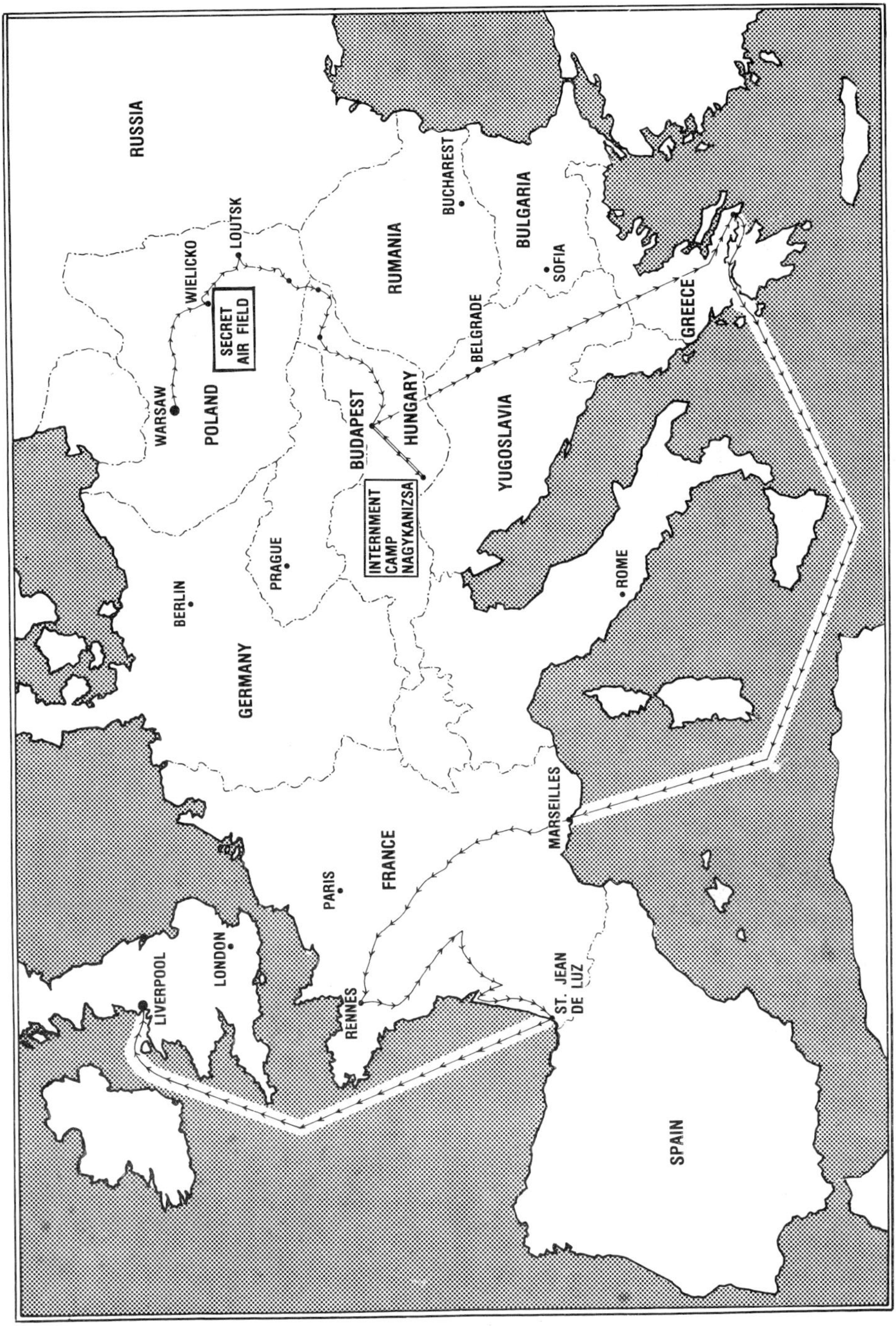
RUSSIA
LOUTSK
WIELICKO
SECRET AIR FIELD
WARSAW
POLAND
BUCHAREST
BULGARIA
RUMANIA
SOFIA
BELGRADE
GREECE
BUDAPEST
HUNGARY
YUGOSLAVIA
INTERNMENT CAMP NAGYKANIZSA
PRAGUE
BERLIN
GERMANY
ROME
MARSEILLES
FRANCE
PARIS
LONDON
LIVERPOOL
RENNES
ST. JEAN DE LUZ
SPAIN

Ox-Box On Brown Knoll

Airspeed Oxford IWM

Oxford HN594 of 21 Advanced Flying Unit, Seighford, on a map reading exercise crashed on Brown Knoll, December 28, 1945. Map reference 082852.

The volume of air traffic over the British Isles during the early war years caused the birth of the Empire Air Training Scheme. Far away from the congestion, the relatively empty skies of Canada, New Zealand, Australia and South Africa were ideal training spaces for the aircrews of the RAF.

There was, however, one big disadvantage, the crews sent abroad and trained in the clear blue skies of the Dominions returned to this country to face the heavy cloud-choked skies of England, Scotland and Wales. It was found necessary to form special units to acclimatise the crews to the notorious European weather conditions — these were known as the AFU's (Advanced Flying Units).

Inevitably, flying accidents occurred usually over high ground as "Empire" trained pilots failed to cope with the low overcast which forever seemed to hang over the country. This is the story of one such flying accident.

Flying an aircraft under power into the ground usually meant the deaths of the occupants, but when Oxford HN 594 of No. 21 AFU smashed into Brown Knoll in Derbyshire and disintegrated, the crew of three survived. The least injured of them, Flying Officer Croker, dragged himself the best way that he could over desolate moorland for over a mile to raise the alarm.

The last flight of Oxford HN 594 was a routine affair — a simple map reading exercise. Flying Officers Croker and Dowthwaite had returned from South Africa earlier in the year and were on a course at Seighford, near Stafford. Converting from single engined aircraft to multi-engined, RAF pilots usually took their first step with the light twin-engined Ansons or Oxfords.

That summer had seen the end of the war in Europe and the Far East — the date was December 28th, 1945.

It was a dark showery day with the inevitable low cloud providing a ten tenths cover stretching beyond the parked Airspeed Oxford to the airfield perimeter and on into the distance.

It was Friday after lunch that the three men, wearing their parachutes, walked unhurriedly towards the trainer. They appeared ill-equipped for flying in the middle of an English winter for they wore no heavy flying clothing, instead they were dressed in their blue battledress uniforms. As they were on a cross-country map reading exercise they would be flying low, so avoiding the freezing conditions experienced at higher altitudes. Also the Oxford cabins were heated — it would be a reasonably short comfortable trip — so they reasoned. It was a decision that they would later regret as they lay amidst shattered wood and metal on the snow covered peakland.

Warrant Officer "Robbie" Robinson was a pilot, navigation instructor, who was there to put the two Flying Officers through a map reading test. The route that he intended to take was well known to him, for he lived in the Sheffield area. For him the trip was very much routine.

The three scrambled into the "Ox-box", as that particular aircraft type was slang-named. HN 594 was an aircraft that was then getting on in years, but was still well suited to the role it played, just so long as no strenuous demands were made upon it.

John Dowthwaite took up the first pilot's position (the left hand seat). He had been married on his return from South Africa in the July of that year and on this occasion was wearing his best, new black leather shoes, which he had worn last on his wedding day. The smart blue uniform that he wore had been a wedding present from his wife.

He pulled on his flying helmet and turned to his instructor for course directions.

Robinson pulled out a map from a pocket situated by a folding map table, settled in the second pilot's position and proceeded to mark out a triangular, three leg course. Because this was done whilst in the aircraft, no one at Seighford knew the flight path that HN 594 had taken.

Ted Croker took up the third position on the seat behind the other two, situated on the main spar, he would be a passenger for the first leg of the flight. Years later he was to become a league footballer and play for Charlton. Eventually he would be appointed as Secretary of the Football Association. But then, on that Friday afternoon in December, he and John Dowthwaite had to convince "Robbie" that they could follow his pencil lines scrawled across that grubby map.

At a rough guess it looked like a 140 mile round trip. A couple of hours should see them back at Seighford again.

Control gave them clearance for take-off and John Dowthwaite opened the throttles, the two Cheetah engines roared to full power and after what seemed like a good deal of runway had been used up, they were in the air and heading north east on the first leg of the triangular flight path.

The twin-engined trainer plodded along at a mere 1,000 feet keeping below the dull overcast with John Dowthwaite picking out landmarks and keeping to a compass bearing.

As the ground began to rise on approach to the Pennines, the cloud seemed to be descending to cling to the hills. A further glance at the map told Dowthwaite that the ground on their flight path rose to over 2,088 feet — he would have to climb.

A tug on his arm; Robbie Robinson, the instructor, was motioning to him to change

'Robbie' Robinson

places with Ted Croker. With the visibility deteriorating fast Dowthwaite was relieved to hand over at this stage.

Robinson in the second pilot's position took control as the other two exchanged places. It was about time to change onto the next leg and he began to execute a series of steep turns in order to locate the start of the second leg. As Dowthwaite left his seat he stabbed a finger at a spot-height in their vicinity, indicating the danger to Robinson.

Ted Croker settled into the pilot's position and surveyed the black cloud swirling about the cockpit. Occasional glimpses of dark hills sporting patches of snow did nothing to ease his mind.

Biting his nails in mock terror he turned to Dowthwaite. The situation they were in was a far cry from the clear, sun-drenched skies of South Africa.

Down to the business at hand and Croker spread out the map on his knees and looked at their course — Kinderscout 2,088 feet! A glance at the altimeter told him that they

John Dowthwaite

Ted Croker

would be in trouble if they didn't cram some space under that plane. They needed two to three hundred feet immediately.

Tilting the map towards Robinson, Croker tapped the point on the map where the spot-height on Kinderscout was indicated.

Robinson nodded and called out above the sound of the engines: "It's all right! I know this country like the back of my hand." So saying he pulled back the control column, opened up the throttles and began to nudge the Ox-box up through the cloud blanket.

It seemed to Croker that the old aircraft was struggling. The rev. counters were showing too slow a build up. Airspeed indicator appeared to be stuck — they were making very little headway in that steady climb. Definitely the old Ox-box was "clapped out" he decided. Glancing out at the port wing he saw that ice was building up along the leading edge — that wouldn't help matters. He was in no hurry to take over the controls at this point from Robbie — who appeared to be unflappable.

At around one hundred miles per hour the Oxford struck the top of Brown Knoll, Derbyshire. Skidding and bouncing HN 594 smashed itself to pieces coming to rest some 150 feet from the point of impact.

It was about 2.30 in the afternoon.

As Croker regained consciousness he decided that he was having a particularly bad dream and promptly did his best to fall asleep again — maybe the cold would go away.

The sound of moaning brought him fully round. Easing himself up he saw that he had been flung some distance from the aircraft. He recalled that after he had changed places with Dowthwaite he had not got around to strapping himself in. Had he been firmly secured to his seat he would now be lying amidst that shattered heap of twisted wreckage.

At this stage Croker was mildly surprised to find himself with what appeared to be light injuries, just a dull pain in each ankle. The pain became more intense as he limped over to where the other two were lying amidst the splintered wood and metal that had once formed a warm comfortable cockpit.

Above and facing page Oxford HN594 taken at the time of the crash.

Of the two, Croker could see that Robinson was the more seriously injured. His jaw was broken and there were leg and internal injuries.

A few feet away Dowthwaite lay on his back with a badly-smashed left leg.

Still half-convinced that it was all reality Croker began making his two companions as comfortable as he could. None of them was adequately dressed to withstand the freezing December conditions for any length of time.

Taking the parachutes that had burst open on impact, Croker wrapped the two men up in them.

"Is it a dream or is it real?" muttered Croker to no one in particular.

"It is real right enough," answered Dowthwaite as he began to recover consciousness.

"We are off track . . . an air search will have problems finding us," said Croker, "and it will be dark soon, he added, glancing round the desolate moorland.

Croker and Dowthwaite reasoned out their plight. A night on the moors in the depth of winter was a grim prospect. An air search would be made when they became overdue, but that would not be until next day. It could be days before they were eventually found, they decided.

Croker made up his mind — he would have to go for help, but which way to go? If he chose the wrong direction he could end up wandering for miles.

"Which way do I go?" He enquired hopefully of Dowthwaite.

Waving his arm vaguely in the direction of their flight path Johnny Dowthwaite muttered: "That way!"

Croker knew that his friend was just guessing.

"Which way do I go Robbie?" After all the Sheffielder had said that he knew this area like the back of his hand.

The instructor mumbled something, through a jaw that was later found to be broken in seven places, indicating a route off the moor.

Shaking his head, Croker decided to ignore both directions given to him and instead to follow a strong instinctive feeling.

After sheltering his two companions the best way that he could, he set off through the mist and snow.

He found that he could no longer bear the weight on his ankles and began to crawl and shuffle his way across the moor. He soon became soaking wet from the snow, and the water froze against his skin. The cold was becoming unbearable especially when he stopped his exertions for brief rests.

Ahead of him he could see some sheep, adequately protected against the elements by their thick woollen coats. If only he could get near enough to one of them, he could catch it and get some warmth from its body.

The sight of a bedraggled human being crawling on all fours towards them out of the mist did nothing for the peace of mind of those

hardy creatures and they bounded off taking their warmth with them.

Croker pressed on and after a while the ground began to slope away, so that he could slither along on his bottom.

The light was fading as he came across a valley with a stream running across it . . . and, in the distance, two houses.

Smoke from one of the chimneys reassured the injured airman that the buildings were inhabited and he began to crawl painfully towards them. He could no longer feel his legs and feet as he dragged himself through the icy stream and up a banking.

There was a Youth Hostel Association sign on the side of the nearest building and as he got close a man emerged and began walking away from it. However, he failed to hear Croker's cries for help as he disappeared into the dusk.

Eventually he reached the YHA door and hammered on it with his frozen hands — there was no reply. Painfully, he struggled round to the adjoining building and once again knocked hard.

Mrs. Shirt opened her front door and gasped. In the half-light a bedraggled figure crouched on her doorstep. He had no shoes on his feet, no top coat or hat; his clothes were soaked and torn.

The RAF wings over the man's left breast pocket told all — the hills had claimed yet another victim. It was becoming an almost common occurrence and her house was in the front line, situated as it was high up the valley towards Edale Head.

Once inside Croker shivered by the fireside and gasped out his story. Mrs. Shirt would have to go down to the village of Edale to get help — it was about a mile down the valley. Before she left she asked him if there was anything that he wanted.

"Just a bowl of hot water for my feet," he said through chattering teeth.

With his feet in that luscious hot water Ted Croker passed out.

Night closed in on the two figures wrapped in parachutes lying among the broken remains of HN 594.

Robbie was calling weakly for help for what seemed like hours to Johnny Dowthwaite who lay a short distance from him. It was terribly cold, if only he could crawl nearer to Robbie they could keep each other warm through the night.

John tried to move but his legs stubbornly refused to obey his commands. Reaching down he felt his limbs and discovered his shin bone protruding through the skin of his left leg. Didn't ought to be sticking out like that, he reasoned and he attempted to push it back where it belonged and fell unconscious.

Leading the search and rescue Flt.-Lt. Crichton.

It was dark as members of the Mountain Rescue Team lifted the unconscious pilot into the ambulance which was parked outside the YHA. They had to bring him round so that he could give them the whereabouts of the wreck and the other two airmen.

Now that he was warm and comfortable Croker fought to keep himself awake so that he could answer the questions put to him by the search party. But it was hopeless, try as he might he could not give them the exact direction and position of HN 594.

For nine hours, search parties dragging sledges behind them scoured thousands of acres of moors, intermittently flooding the area with light from flares.

After losing one of their sledges over a ravine the rescue teams finally called a halt at 10 p.m. The chances of coming across the two men in the pitch darkness was remote. The search would commence again at first light.

At day break RAF planes assisted in the search and the wreckage was eventually spotted at about 10.30 a.m. The previous night's search had taken one rescue party to within 400 yards of the two men.

After 20 hours lying in the open Robbie Robinson and Johnny Dowthwaite were carried about a mile and a half across the moor and taken to an RAF hospital at Wilmslow, Cheshire, where because of frost-bite and loss of blood Robinson had to have a leg amputated.

Ted Croker had made that same journey, the shortest way off the moor, in about two hours with two injured ankles. "Not bad going," he later reasoned.

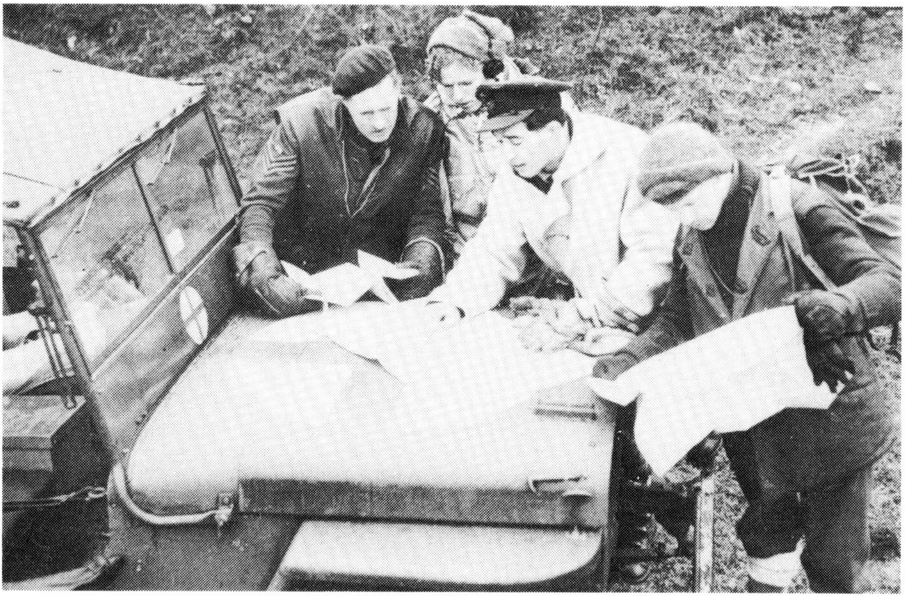

Photographs taken at the time, Mountain Rescue personel receive their instructions from 'Doc' Crichton. 'We're on our way!' A signal rocket is discharged by the rescue team from the road outside the Y.H.A. next to Lee House.

By 1945 the Mountain Rescue Service was receiving the equipment to carry out their difficult job. The versatile American Jeep was the ideal vehicle for traversing the moorland. When the crash was located first aid was given to the two injured airmen.

'Easy does it' Doc. Crichton picks out a route across the moor with either Robinson or Dowthwaite on the stretcher.

The final barrier, a fast running stream, is crossed, just a short distance to the ambulance.

One of the Oxford's Cheetah engines, recovered from the moor in 1972 by cadets and staff of 1196 Romiley ATC Sqn. and is now at their H.Q. at Romiley, near Stockport.

In March 1981 Football Association Secretary Ted Croker revisited the site of his accident on Brown Knoll.

Acting as guide to the site Mr. Ron Collier, aviation historian and author (left) Ted Croker (centre) Barnsley Chronicle writer artist Roni Wilkinson (right) standing amidst the small amounts of wreckage that remain.

Ted Croker attempts to identify some of the pieces. He is here examining one of the radiators that was once located in the leading edge of the Oxford's wing.

After retracing the route that he once covered on his hands and knees Ted arrives at the gate of Lee House where 36 years ago he crawled through on his hands and knees.

Oxford Trainer GIPSON

Even The Best

Oxford NM683 of Pathfinder Navigational Training Unit, Warboys, on a map reading exercise to Stretton, crashed on Rushup Edge, March 4, 1945. Map reference 116837.

The Pathfinder Force came into being on the August 15th, 1942 and was to spearhead the Bomber Command's annihilation of German cities for three years. Its crew members were volunteers and were selected carefully from applicant crews.

Standards were of the highest and the Commander of the elite force, Group Captain Donald Bennett, was a hard taskmaster who ordered the return of any crew that failed to make the grade.

Pathfinder aircraft arrived at the target first dropping coloured markers for the main Force bomb aimers to aim at. Accurate navigation and timing were essential with the Pathfinder pilots maintaining a correct course and airspeed in varying flying conditions.

Not only had the Pathfinder crews to be determined in pressing on to the target, but they had also to be "unflappable" types who could be trusted to drop their target indicators only when they had identified the area to be bombed. Wrongly placed TI's meant a wasted trip for the main Force bombers who followed them in.

Every crew member's job had to be known to the "Skipper" so that he could make correct decisions and he had to be above average at his own job. In particular, it was necessary for him to be a good navigator who could map-read from some height. It was at his command only that the target indicators were dropped. Success or failure of a bombing raid depended upon the skill of the Pathfinder pilots.

On the raid by 617 Squadron on the German Dams, the use was made of a Master Bomber. W/Commander Guy Gibson circuited the target and directed the individual attacks of each aircraft. That method was thereafter used by the Pathfinder Force. Of the Master Bomber "Flight Magazine" of 9th March, 1946 commented:

"Only men of proven ability possessing the qualities of leadership, flexibility of outlook, clear judgement and capable of immediate reaction to changed circumstances were selected for the job." Such were the pilots of the elite Pathfinder Force, who were chosen to become Master Bombers.

On March 4th, 1945, an experienced Pathfinder pilot and Master Bomber flying an Oxford trainer flew into the hillside above the Vale of Edale. After completing a double tour of operations with Pathfinder Force, earning the Distinguished Flying Cross and Bar, Flight Lieutenant Brian Gipson, having survived the flak and fighters over Germany, had fallen victim to the notorious Dark Peak Hills.

With the rapidly changing conditions and hill-hugging cloud masses, the Pennine hills of north Derbyshire are no respecter of skilled fliers.

Upon returning from Canada where he had trained as a pilot, Brian Gipson moved on to 1667 Heavy Conversion Unit at Faldingworth, where he first made contact with the Pathfinders. It was a recruiting drive by a pilot from that recently-formed Group that caught his imagination and, with his crew's permission, he volunteered immediately.

After completing training on four-engined aircraft, he (along with his crew) moved to the Pathfinder Navigational Training Unit at Upwood. After a week of intensive training including cross-country flights, he and his crew were rejected. Disappointed, they moved to a Squadron in the Main Force, 576 Squadron, based at Elsham Wolds. It was here that Brian Gipson made his first ever trip over Germany and found it all rather exciting.

In order to give new pilots experience, they alone of the crew flew as passenger with an experienced crew on one sortie. The target for 1st January 1944 was Berlin — and along he went as second pilot and very much a novice. Take off was four minutes past midnight.

As the Lancaster approached the target over Berlin, he was able to observe what was going on all around. He looked on with calm interest as tracer shells lashed past the cockpit. A Focke-Wulf FW 190 was intent on knocking them out of the skies, but they dodged that particular attack. They were attacked on two other occasions, however, by nightfighters, as they left the target area.

Returning, the pilot, Flight Sergeant Thomas, got off track and flew over the flak defences at Frankfurt — both starboard engines began to leak fuel as shrapnel laced the wing.

For some reason, Flight Sergeant Thomas thought that they were under attack by fighters and he went into a steep dive. That dive seemed to be going on far too long for the crew and they began yelling for the skipper to pull out of it. The pilot was heaving back on the control column as hard as he could and cried out "I can't!"

Reaching across, Brian Gipson grabbed the stick and heaved it back with the Skipper — the airspeed indicator had gone right around the clock and the Lancaster must have reached around 300 m.p.h. in that dive. When the two pilots had managed to pull out of the dive, they were only a few thousand feet up.

They arrived back at Elsham Wolds with crew exhausted and shaken by their ordeal, but because it was Brian's first operational flight, he considered it an everyday event that every flight over Germany was like that and found it in no way nerve-racking — in fact, he thought it very exciting!

Brian Gipson

The following month, however, on a raid — this time to Schweinfurt, piloting his own aircraft, he went through another experience which was to test his flying skills to the limit — and it was not caused by any enemy action.

On the night of February 24th, 1944, a total force of 734 bombers set out to bomb factories where airframes were being manufactured, at Schweinfurt.

Gipson and his crew were running twelve minutes late so rather than climb to the altitude of the rest of the bomber stream, he decided to catch up at the expense of gaining height.

Even at that altitude the rear turret froze up on the way out and would not operate. As they approached the target they could see fires blazing below. Above them, illuminated by the fires, they could see other aircraft making their bomb runs. As they watched above the crew could see a bomber passing above them from port to starboard — its bomb doors open. Directly above them, it dropped its deadly bomb load . . . Gipson slipped the Lancaster sideways but was too late! One bomb struck the port inner spinner, another plunged through the starboard wing in-board of number one fuel tank. A third passed clean through the fuselage close to the mid-upper gun turret. The Wireless Operator was sent back to examine the damage caused by this third bomb — he was advised to take a torch. It was good advice — for the poor Sparks almost stepped into space through a gaping hole torn by the bomb.

Undaunted, Gipson carried on to bomb the target with the port inner propellor feathered. Once the bomb load had gone, he attempted to re-trim the Lancaster — only to find that the trimmer had frozen. As a result of this, he had to fly home with one foot jammed against the control column exerting force to keep his aircraft stable.

Problems continued for them as the intercom packed up. The crew was unable to communicate for instruction and course changes, so these had to be scribbled on bits of paper.

Then the 1196 (pilot's speech transmitter) packed up. After 8 hours 35 minutes they were safely home — thanks to some expert flying by the Skipper.

The very next night they were sent to Augsberg to continue wrecking aircraft factories. Over the target Gipson's Lancaster got conned by searchlights and he had to take evasive action. This was to be the longest trip for he and his crew, 8 hours 50 minutes. The ancient city was devastated as was the modern industrial area.

An attempt to send the exhausted crews of 576 Squadron on another raid the following night was thwarted at briefing by the medical officer, who ordered them to their beds.

Gipson kept up his clamour to join the Pathfinder Force and at last he and his crew received a posting to Navigational Training Unit at Upwood. Now that they were a fully-blooded experienced aircrew, they were successful in completing the course and received a posting to 156 Pathfinder Squadron.

Some measure of the expertise that they had accrued as a team can be seen in the first Pathfinder raid they took part in.

Target for March 24th-25th, 1944 was Berlin — and it was to prove a costly one. The planners had hoped that the enemy might mistake the target to be Stettin and send the fighters there — but this did not happen. The route back took bombers to the Rhur Valley area and the heavy defences — many bombers drifted over those areas and were destroyed.

Flying with the bombers carrying markers (new crews weren't allowed to carry target markers) as supporting bombers in advance of the Main Force, Gipson's crew experienced difficulties before the coast of Denmark. The Gee navigational aid became inoperative and they could have turned back but were keen to do well on their first raid with the Pathfinders. They pressed on using dead reckoning — it was too cloudy above them to obtain an astral fix. They assumed that they had crossed Denmark and the navigator said that it was time to turn, then again later as they approached Stettin. After calculating the known wind and speed and time, the Navigator confidently announced that they were over Berlin.

Nothing stirred on the earth beneath them — all was dark and silent — where had they arrived? Where exactly WERE they?

Suddenly, the rear gunner called out: "Skipper! All hell's let loose at the back!"

They had crossed the North Sea, Denmark, made the scheduled course changes all on dead reckoning — and arrived over Berlin a minute and a half early! An excellent display of precision flying by anyone's standards. Behind them the other Pathfinders had begun marking and the supporting Pathfinders had begun to bomb.

Realising the danger of making a tight turn and heading back to the target centre with upwards of 1000 bombers flying towards them, Gipson decided to make a large circuit and join the bomber stream from behind. When they finally arrived over that target and began their bombing run, they were on their own over the German capital, everyone else had gone home . . . They dropped their bombs on the fires burning below — and turned for home themselves.

Meanwhile, a 60 miles wide swathe of bombers thundered back across Germany making for England. The German nightfighters rose to the occasion and began attacking individual aircraft. Around ninety failed to return.

For Gipson and crew, however, it was the quietest trip they ever made and they returned unscathed without seeing flak or fighters. So ended their first flight with the Pathfinders.

Just three months later Flight Lieutenant Gipson was chosen as Master Bomber, which was an indication of his progress as a pilot and navigator and the skill of his crew — all welded together as a complete team under their Skipper.

Invasion of Europe had taken place on the 6th of June and Hitler was launching his V weapons at the bridgeheads in France and at London. Underground storage places for Hitler terror weapons at Wizernes in France were the targets. It was a daylight raid made by 200 bombers — leading the way and directing the attack — Brian Gipson.

He had just arrived over the target when a flak burst knocked the engine sump off the starboard inner engine — causing smoke to pour out. He eventually got the fire out and carried on to mark the target, then he stayed around to direct the bombing by the Main Force. When the bombers had turned for home, Gipson limped after them on three engines — the last to leave the target area. They were so late getting back that they had been reported shot down . . . That attack of Wizernes was the most successful ever carried out on a doodlebug centre. The Germans had cunningly concealed their terror weapons deep beneath the innocent open fields — but Gipson had located that underground store-place, marked it, and directed every bomber to drop its load on the right spot.

Later that day, a photographic reconnaissance aircraft took shots of the damage — the entire centre of the field had been completely caved in.

The next most demanding trip was a raid on Essen in October of 1944. Again, things went wrong from the start. They hit a bad weather front over the continent and immediately the windscreen iced up — the de-icer refused to function — and this was followed by the failure of the H2S set (this was the blind bombing aid — so if the 10-10ths cloud persisted to the target they would be unable to drop their sky markers) code-named Wanganui. Static electricity in the clouds played havoc with the instruments, yet they ploughed on and reached Essen after 1 hour 10 minutes blind flying. They dropped their bombs and were hit by flak as they left the target area. As they began to circuit the home field, they discovered that the undercarriage would not lower and consequently, they had to blow the wheels down with emergency air (the hydraulics had been punctured).

Brian Gipson at the controls of an Oxford trainer.

Another trip to Essen later that year completed the required tour of ops and brought the award of bar to the DFC for Gipson. The citation runs:
"Since being recommended for the Distinguished Flying Cross, he has completed an extended tour of operations in the most exemplary manner. He has always shown a high order of skill, courage and determination and his crew has achieved a high standard of target marking over a long period. This was largely due to the fine leadership, courage and enthusiasm of Flight Lieutenant Gipson."

How then did such a skilled and experienced pilot come to smash an aircraft into the hillside in Derbyshire — in broad daylight?

The dangerous terrain of the Pennine chain of hills has been stated many times. In the war years, however, the true nature of that area was only just beginning to register with the authorities as the conflict in Europe drew to a close. The high ground had claimed numerous victims — and Flight Lieutenant Gipson was one of many.

After completing his tour and receiving the bar to his DFC, along with the award of the permanent Pathfinder Badge, he moved to the Pathfinder Navigational Training Unit at Warboys as an Instructor. It was March 1945, Germany was being squeezed on two fronts and the end was near. To Brian Gipson it seemed that the worst was over and, posted as he was a short distance from home at Chatteris, things looked bright for him. He settled down to his task as Instructor.

Because of the change in certain duties on Pathfinder bombers, the Unit at Warboys was engaged in the training of engineers as map readers. Consequently, an Oxford was supplied for the job — Oxford NM 683. Gipson was one of the few pilots on the staff who was qualified to fly the twin-engined trainer, so he frequently got the job.

It didn't take long for the Instructors to realise that the map reading trips had no flight plan and that they could arrange to take people going on leave to their nearest aerodrome.

It was a beautiful day, March 4th, 1945, and Flight Lieutenant Jones was going on leave. The nearest aerodrome for him was Stretton, Cheshire. The excuse for this trip was the training of Flying Officer Skone-Reese. Flight Lieutenant Barclay was the navigation instructor and Brian Gipson was at the controls. All four were holders of the DFC — and all were most experienced and capable Pathfinder personnel.

It was around lunchtime when the four of them took off. Unlike the Lancaster the Oxford carried no navigational aids — but there was little cloud about. Jones sat facing the tail and was reading a book — his helmet intercom was not connected — he didn't want to be disturbed by the occasional banter of the other three.

As the Oxford approached the Pennine range, the cloud base began to get lower and Gipson kept below it. The ground was rising gently to meet the clouds and Gipson noted that the altimeter was showing 1,000 feet — the aircraft was moving into a sandwich that was closing up.

Eventually, Gipson found that he was flying up a valley with cloud covered hills on either side. Suddenly the valley came to a dead end as a steep wooded slope went up into the clouds. He pulled back on the control column, opened the throttle and powered up through the cloud. An expanse of white and grey spread out before him — they had no navigational aids and they didn't know where they were. Gipson checked the fuel gauges

A view of the business end of the Oxford.

and they were close to zero. He reached out and switched on the two emergency tanks — but nothing happened.

"Something's going to have to happen soon — we're coming down anyway!" he said as he worked at the petrol cocks, trying to get them to function.

"We should be clear of the Pennines by now," exclaimed Barclay who had taken on the responsibility of navigation.

"Better that we go down under control than risk having to glide down when the engines pack in," replied Gipson.

Losing 200 feet per minute, he gently eased the Oxford down through the cloud. At the last second, Gipson saw the ground and yelled out — pulling back on the stick with all his might. That was the last thing he remembered.

The Oxford struck the ground a glancing blow and the wings broke, bending backwards. The cockpit was shattered and the contents spilled out over the hillside.

It was raining heavily as Brian Gipson regained consciousness. There was what seemed to be a deathly hush — after the noise roar of the two Cheetah radial engines but he could hear a buzzing sound which he recognised as the giro running down — then he heard a faint groan.

He could recall someone lifting him from the wreckage and carrying him to a fire engine. Then he remembered being inside a farmhouse — and attempting to communicate with a policeman — telling him to get in touch with RAF Warboys. The next thing he recollected were the warm sheets and blankets of the hospital bed at the RAF Hospital at Wilmslow. His injuries consisted of a badly-cut face and a broken right ankle. One of the others had a fractured backbone, but he was up and about before Gipson was and shortly left the hospital.

A few remains of the NM683 clinging to the hillside.

In April 1945 he was posted back to 582 Squadron — never to fly again operationally.

Since leaving the RAF, Gipson has held a variety of jobs. He was a dispenser for the local doctors for 10 years, then became a schoolteacher teaching woodwork at Cromwell Community College, Chatteris, for 20 years. He worked for a time as a carpenter for a boat building firm and has since retired.

In 1967, a painful swelling appeared on his left hand. An X-ray in hospital showed up a foreign body and an operation was performed to remove it. After the operation, the offending object was given to Gipson as a souvenir — it was quite obviously a corner off one of the instruments from the Oxford NM 683. A painful reminder of the crash on Rushup Edge, on the Pennine hills in Derbyshire, a range of hills which are no respecter of persons and will take to itself even the best.

Mr. Gipson in 1981 with his Distinguished Flying Cross and certificate for the award of The Permanent Pathfinder Badge. Which was of more value to pilots than the D.F.C. because fewer of them were given.

IWM

Anson N9912 of 25 Operational Training Unit, crashed on Whitwell Moor, Bolsterstones, March 31, 1942 when the wireless transmitter failed and the aircraft got off track. The crew of four escaped serious injury.
Map reference 249976.

OWNSWORTH

IWM

Wellington R1011, of 28 Operational Training Unit flying on a night exercise from Wymeswold crashed on Birchen Bank Moss, January 30th, 1943. Map reference 097978.

On the night of the 29th, six Wellington 1C's took off in succession on a Command Bullseye exercise. The crews were nearing the end of their training as bomber crews and would shortly be posted to squadrons engaged in operations.

The trip that night would especially test the abilities of the navigator, Pilot Officer Grisdale, who had the task of directing the bomber on a circuitous course that would take them far north to Scotland and back to base at Wymeswold in Leicestershire. A trip that had been estimated to take from six and a half to seven hours.

The purpose behind flights of such long duration was to ready RAF crews for similiar length sorties to German cities.

The weather had been poor all day and got worse during the night. Out of the six Wellingtons taking part in the exercise, two crashed killing crew members. Wellington R1538 crashed at Lonton near Stoke-on-Trent, two died and two were injured.

R1011 dropped through cloud at around 1.45 a.m. and hit the moorland above the A628 road, near Woodhead, killing the pilot, Flying Officer Lane and two other crew members, Pilot Officer Brown and Sergeant Rouse.

The navigator, Grisdale and the rear gunner Sergeant R. S. Miller survived and were later admitted to Ashton hospital suffering from exposure.

It was the considered opinion of the commanding officer at 28 OTU that he had lost the best crew of number seven course with the crash of R1011.

Oxford LX 518, on a night training flight from Wheaton Aston crashed on Margery Hill, October 19th, 1943. Map reference 184967.

For Pilot Officer Kyne it was to be his first solo night flight. He had commenced flying in Oxfords in September, 1943 and had amassed a total of 14 hours 20 minutes flying time on that type. He was assessed by his instructor as an 'average pilot'.

It had reached that point in his training where he had to fly at night on his own. They had just landed after flying over the exact course that he was about to attempt on his own.

During the flight with his instructor the various drome lights and beacons had been pointed out. The flight had been an easy one and Kyne had carried it out successfully. Instruments and radio had all functioned well, as had the two Cheetah engines. There was two and a half hours flying time in the three fuel tanks — all seemed well.

Before take-off for his solo flight he received a careful briefing. Taking off from the base at Wheaton Aston he was to head west 20 miles to Condover, where he was to turn due north to Shawbury, a distance of about seven miles. Once over the drome at Shawbury he would turn due east and head back to Wheaton Aston — a round trip of fifty miles over a triangular course.

The briefing included aids to "Lost Procedure"; should Kyne lose his way to any of the three dromes then he had recourse to various systems then in operation, such as 'Pundit' (code letters flashed by individual airfields) or 'Darkie' (a radio emergency system) IFF, Identification Friend or Foe transmitter; searchlight homing and a system known as 'Occult'.

Before take-off the instructor asked Kyne if he had any questions on Lost Procedure, the trainee answered in the negative.

The instructor left the aircraft and watched as the trainee pilot took off into the night — it was 8.45 p.m.

After gaining height over the airfield, Kyne called up on the R/T using the code name for Wheaton, 'Banet White' and declared that he was setting course for 'Bureau' (code name for Condover). It was the last that was seen or

heard of Kyne and LX 518 until their grim discovery on Margery Hill, on the boundary of West Yorkshire and Derbyshire.

Twenty minutes after take-off and personnel at Ground Control, Wheaton became concerned as the weather suddenly began to deteriorate. By 9.45 p.m. it was drizzling and a call went out for all training aircraft to return.

At 9.10 p.m. the beacon at Shawbury failed and remained out of action for over an hour — during that time Kyne vanished.

Two Oxford trainers became overdue and 'Overdue Action' was taken at 12.10 a.m. One landed safely at Wrexham, but no word was heard from LX518.

On October 23rd, at 12 noon, the wreckage was discovered. Kyne had been killed instantly as his aircraft had ploughed into the moorland under power.

It was assumed that Kyne had become lost soon after take-off and for some reason failed to carry out any of the correct procedure for such an emergency. He must have gradually drifted in a north easterly direction, then decided to drop through the cloud to establish his position.

Even the Royal Observer Corps had failed to track the errant Oxford which must have crashed sometime after midnight over 40 miles from its planned triangular course in the west midlands.

Possible Fi 103 (V1) explosion site. Map reference 186965.

A mystery surrounds the cause of a large blast area on a flat stretch of moorland on Margery Hill. Thick gauge aluminium sheeting is to be found at the spot. If they are the remains of a German flying bomb then it seems likely that it was one of 50 that were launched from Heinkel 111's over the North Sea.

On December 24th, 1944, according to the book "Flying Bomb" by Richard Anthony Young, 50 Heinkels air-launched their V1's in an area between Bridlington and Skegness. Just before dawn thirty of the 'Divers' (as they were code named) crossed the East Coast headed for Manchester. Only one managed it all the way and crashed in the city killing 37 people and injuring 67 others. Eleven bombs came within 15 miles of the aiming point and six fell as close as six miles from Manchester city centre.

The remains on Margery Hill may be fragments from one of the eleven. Information is still being sought on the remains at this site.

BRIAN R. ROBINSON

Tiger Moth T6164 of 24 Elementary Flying Training School, crashed April 12, 1945, above Chew Brook whilst on a two hour cross country training flight. The pilot, M. A. O'Connell, a New Zealander, was killed outright.
Map reference 034015.

H. HOLMES
Mustang 472181, 336 Fighter Squadron, flown by Frederick crashed same day as Wilhoit, near Crewe

Mustang P51D of 336 Fighter Squadron U.S.A.A.F. flying from Debden to Speke, crashed at Glossop, May 29, 1945. Private ground.

336 had initially been a R.A.F. squadron designated 133, one of the three fighter units known as 'Eagle Squadrons' and flown by American volunteer pilots. With the entry of the United States into the European war the three volunteer squadrons, 71, 121 and 133 became 334, 335 and 336 respectively. They were known as the 4th Fighter Group "The Eagles" the official transfer taking place on September 29th, 1942.

The same month that the war in Europe ended 336 Fighter Squadron lost two aircraft on the same day on a routine cross country flight.

On Tuesday morning, May 29th, 1945, just 21 days after the war in Europe had ended, 12 Mustangs took off from Debden in Essex, bound for Speke, Liverpool, a distance of 160 miles as the crow flies.

Shortly after take-off at 10 o'clock the fighters encountered bad weather. As they approached the high ground of the Peak District the clouds rose from the hills to a height of 7,000 feet. Two of the red-nosed fighters turned back for base. The others pressed on blindly through the clouds and began to get split up.

Lieutenant Brooker kept the Mustang in front of him in sight as they let down through the clouds; he was following Lieutenant Frederick closely when suddenly the aircraft in front of him flew into the ground.

The blast from Frederick's stricken Mustang hurled Brooker's fighter to one side and a wing tip was ripped off, but he managed to keep control and stay in the air. Badly shaken, he turned back for Debden and landed safely.

Eight Mustangs landed at Speke — one was missing.

Upon becoming separated Flight Officer Darnaby H. Wilhoit had got himself over 25 miles east of track. After passing over the highest of the Pennines in that area safely, he came down through the clouds and turned westward.

He must have identified his position somewhere in the region of Longdendale Valley because he came from that direction flying low over the town of Glossop. But all the high ground in the region had not been cleared, there remained a 1,100 feet high range of hills directly in his flight path.

Wilhoit, flying his sleek Mustang at high speed ripped into a field off Monks Road, Glossop. Two mighty explosions brought people running from their houses.

First to reach the blazing wreckage was a boy, Walter Mason, followed by a land girl, Mrs. Alice Walker. Getting as close to the flames as they could they made attempts to smother the fire with earth until they discovered the body of the pilot. Mrs. Walker saw some papers and a New Testament, which she managed to snatch seconds before the flames reached them.

On November 4th, 1945, the pilots of 4th Fighter Group sailed on the Queen Mary for home, minus two of their comrades, who, having survived the war, had succumbed to the terrible English weather.

Fairey Barracuda BRIAN R. ROBINSON

Barracuda MD 963, of Station Flight, Dunino, Scotland, crashed at Redbrook Clough, July 29, 1945. Map reference 024103.

Pilots who flew the Royal Navy Barracuda and who had been used to its predecessors, the Albacores and the stately Swordfish, were often caught out by this replacement monoplane torpedo bomber. It could not be flown with the same casualness as the biplanes that it was superceding. There had been fatalities among pilots of squadrons first receiving the type — the Barracuda had earned for itself a bad reputation.

Royal Navy requirements had resulted in an aircraft of odd appearance. Because observation of the sea beneath was of prime importance the Barracuda's wings were placed high on the fuselage. But this brought its own problems. The tailplane had to be raised to the top of the fin by the designers at Fairy Aviation in order to avoid turbulance from the high, single wing. Because of its high position it required supporting struts, which in turn added to the amount of drag.

Further, high placed wings meant that the aircraft had to have a large undercarriage that could be retracted into the under-wing surfaces. That undercarriage had to be sturdy enough to cope with deck landings on aircraft carriers — more weight!

The Barracuda in flight was unstable and had to be under the pilot's control all the time. The 'pilot's notes' for the awkward looking contraption, under the sub-heading 'High Speed Stall' carried the following warning: "If the aircraft is stalled in a steep turn either wing may drop sharply but recovery is almost immediate when the pressure on the control column is relaxed."

On July 29th, 1945, a Royal Navy Barracuda whilst executing a turn over moorland in the vicinity of Marsden, slipped into the ground killing the only occupant, the pilot, Sub Lieutenant Ambler.

Mr. J. W. Wood, a blacksmith of Bleak Hey Nook near Standage saw the crash take place. It was just after one o'clock in the afternoon, and Mr. Wood was walking across the moors with his dog when he heard an aircraft approaching. He could not see it at first as the clouds were low and there was a ground mist.

Suddenly it appeared through the cloud at a mere 150 feet, went into a turn, a wing dropped and the aircraft plunged into the hillside. A cloud of blue smoke billowed upwards and the Navy plane errupted into a mass of flames.

There was nothing that Mr. Wood could do to save the pilot, who must have been killed instantly. He raced over to the Great Western Hotel, where he telephoned the West Riding Police.

At the crash site, on the very edge of the Peak District, very little remains of the weird looking aircraft, the Barracuda, of which type a story is told. It is said that an American General upon being shown the Barracuda for the first time, took up a close examination, walking round and round it, then standing back he remarked: "That's the finest flying machine that I have ever seen, but it will never replace the airplane."

Aerobatic Flyer

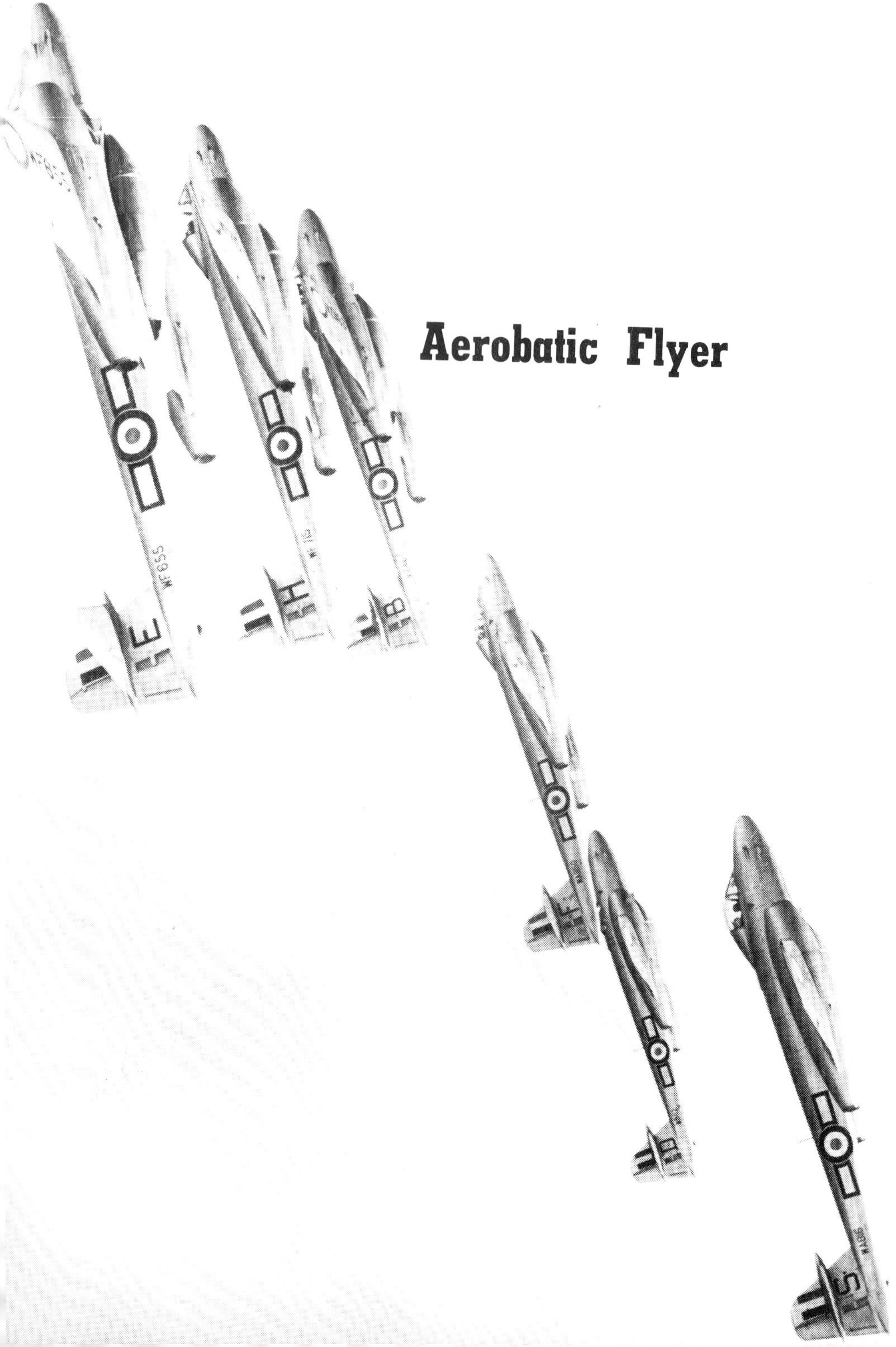

Gloster Meteor BRIAN R. ROBINSON

Meteor RA487 of 66 Fighter Squadron, Linton-on-Ouse, on a night flying exercise, crashed on Hagg Side, December 8, 1950. Map reference 173884.

Crowds throughout Britain are today thrilled by the air displays and incredible aerobatics performed by the world famous Red Arrows, almost always the highlight of any aviation event.

The precision flying programme with its daring high speed manoeuvres has evolved since the last war and the introduction of jet aircraft. Prior to the RAF Red Arrows, flying Hawk trainers which superseded the Folland Gnats, there were the Black Arrows, flying Hawker Hunters and the Blue Diamonds also flying Hawker Hunters.

But an aerobatic team had been thrilling spectators during the early post-war era. No. 66 Squadron flying the first operational jet, the Meteor, pioneer of the jet precision aerobatic teams.

A member of that aero-formation team became lost over Derbyshire and with his fuel gauges registering zero, he baled out. His Meteor Mk 4, still under power, dived into a wooded hillside in the Derwent Valley.

Sergeant Pilot Joseph Harrington joined the RAF in 1943 and was assessed as suitable for pilot training. After introductory training and "useful duty" service, he went to Canada in the spring of 1944 to the flying school. As the war drew to a close, Joe Harrington returned to this country and was given a choice of position — either to serve as a glider pilot or go on a pilot flight engineer course for Lancasters.

Unpowered flight just did not appeal to Joe so he opted for the heavy bombers. After a peacetime tour on Lancasters, he converted to the larger Lincolns and later left the service in 1948.

Civil aviation companies were being swamped by applications from ex-bomber pilots for positions with their companies. An

Joe Harrington

attempt by Joe to continue flying by joining one of the many emerging airlines proved fruitless, ex-Transport Command pilots stood a better chance and picked up the available jobs.

The answer for Joe seemed simple enough — re-enlist as a pilot in Transport Command, then after serving for a period with them try again to join the Civil airlines. In October of 1949 Joe re-enlisted on a four year aircrew engagement — it was a bit drastic! But he dearly wished to be an airline pilot. After a refresher training course, he was assessed as suitable for Transport Command — he had made it.

On June 25th, 1950, North Korean troops crossed the 38th Parallel and advanced into South Korea. RAF fighter squadrons were being strengthened and Joe Harrington found himself on a conversion course to fly the Meteor twin-engined fighter with little say in the matter. So much for Transport Command and eventually, a captain's job with a civil airline!

Joe joined 66 Squadron at Linton-on-Ouse, a fully-fledged fighter pilot. The accident rate was high on the jet squadrons and 66 had its share of fatalities.

Formation aerobatics proved dangerous and on one occasion during a display, Joe Harrington collided with another Meteor over their home base — but fortunately managed to land unscathed.

66 Squadron, however, produced a good formation team under the leadership of Pilot Officer Murphy — and they gave many displays at RAF stations and at "Battle of Britain" week efforts. The way was being paved for the dramatic aerial displays we see today.

It was the winter of that year that the C.O. of 66, Squadron Leader A. Lang, DFC decided to give his men some experience of flying at night. There was the possibility that the Squadron might be called upon to take off in the late evening and return to base to make a night landing.

On December 8th, 1950, Joe took off from Linton. The course he had been given was triangular — he was to fly the first leg to Manchester, then turn due east to a point in East Yorkshire making then a further course change for home base. Simple enough when you can see the ground — but on that particular night, the whole of northern England was covered in a layer of low cloud. The navigation was mainly a matter of steering a heading for a certain time at a constant speed,

FLIGHT MAGAZINE

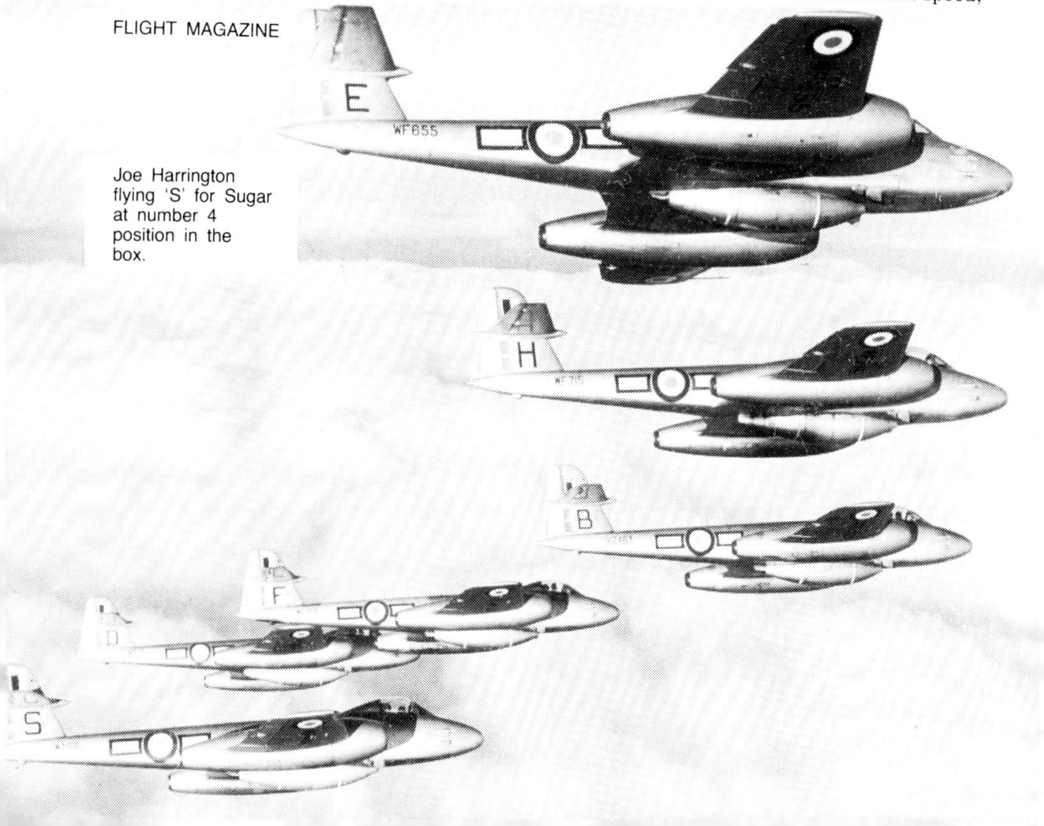

Joe Harrington flying 'S' for Sugar at number 4 position in the box.

with radar service as a back-up.

After the appropriate time lapse, Joe turned the fighter eastwards. He must have been over Manchester — the first leg completed, although he was unable to obtain a visual fix to confirm this.

During the second leg Joe discovered that his 4 channel VHF set had become unserviceable — which meant that he was unable to get radar assistance. By then he should have been at his next course change point — he turned north.

It was no use . . . he had to verify his position. He dropped through the heavy cloud layer and scanned the ground below — nothing!

He was unable to recognise a single feature flashing beneath his aircraft. A glance at the fuel gauge and he knew that he was in serious trouble. He had only minutes left before the twin Derwent engines burnt up the last drops of kerosene.

He switched the IFF set to "distress" although he doubted that any ground station would pick up this signal.

What was he to do now?

A long, straight stretch of road came into sight: he could try to land on that — a better proposition than baling out. He should try to save the aircraft if possible — after all, it had cost the taxpayers plenty. He flew a low pass over the road to warn any possible traffic and also to take a closer inspection.

Suddenly, off the starboard wing tip, a factory chimney loomed into view. That was too close for comfort — he would have to bale out and having made that decision, Joe recalled an incident which had occurred three days before.

The C.O. at Linton-on-Ouse (92 Squadron) had run into trouble and had tried to bale out — and had tragically met his death. The cockpit on the Meteor was well forward, affording the pilot an excellent view all around, but it meant it was a dangerous procedure to attempt to jump from one, with the prospect of being hit by the leading edge of the wing . . .

With this on his mind, Joe ran through all the correct procedures. He would stick to the book — the experts who had set out the prescribed methods had to be trusted.

"I climbed to about 5000 feet, above the cloud, disconnected my headset, throttled back, put down one third flap, trimmed the aircraft then put it into a shallow turn to the left.

"I was halfway out of the cockpit when the aircraft started to descend. I became jammed in that position. The only thing remaining for me to do was to get back into the cockpit and make a second attempt. "I readjusted the trim and climbed onto the seat, jumped, passing over the wing and under the tail — in true text book manner.

"I found myself tumbling through the sky and after several hasty attempts to pull the ripcord, I calmed down as I fell, began to search for it, located it and gave it a good tug!

"As the 'chute opened, blossoming thankfully above me, I recognised even in the blackness, that I was in hilly country — so I prepared myself for landing. I heard an explosion somewhere beneath me . . . I just hoped that the aircraft had crashed in open country.

"My feet touched the ground and I fell flat on my face into what later turned out to be a recently-ploughed field".

After disconnecting his parachute, Joe examined himself and found that he was uninjured, although he was minus one flying boot. His light flying overall was covered in mud and he felt the nip of the December night. Across the fields he could see the lights of a farmhouse twinkling in the distance. He climbed over a fence and limped across the fields.

A middle-aged lady answered the door to Joe's knocking — she looked him up and down

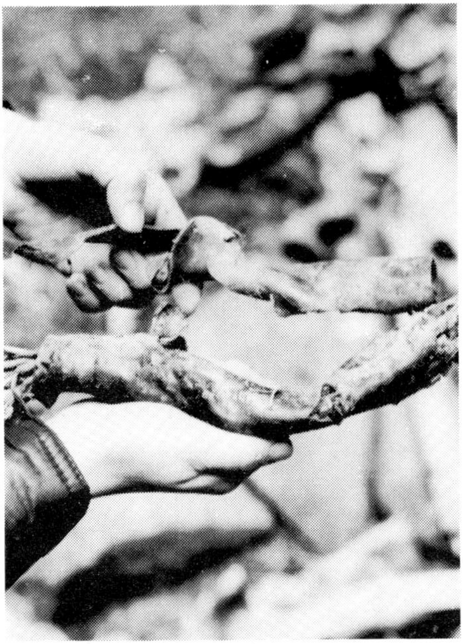

A section of instrument cable with the words "Brake Panel".

and Joe realised that he must have presented quite a strange sight!

"Good evening," he said, determined to reassure her. "I'm sorry to disturb you but I've just had to bale out of my aeroplane and I need help."

"Oh, please — come in and have a cup of tea," responded the woman — as though mud-plastered airmen made a habit of dropping in on her.

Eventually, Joe was taken to the police station at Hope in Derbyshire, where he began to clean himself up. They gave him some soup and after a couple of hours, A RAF Flight Lieutenant arrived to drive him to RAF Finningley where he spent the night.

The following morning, Joe drove back to Linton-on-Ouse where he was given an ovation by the other crew members upon entering the crew room. The only person who seemed put out by Joe's safe arrival was the NCO in charge of the parachute section. The Sergeant should have held on to his ripcord handle and then returned with it — he had let go of it and the handle was lost.

Well, Joe reasoned, you just can't please everyone all of the time!

After completing more than the usual peacetime tour with the fighter squadron, Joe was given the choice of becoming an instructor or doing target towing at Acklington, Northumberland. As that town was not far from his home, he chose the latter course and was posted to Northumberland.

Between his target towing duties flying over the North Sea, Joe was able to study for his civil licence with the eventual aim of achieving his ambition to become a civil aviation pilot.

Joe Harrington, at the time of writing, is a Captain with Swissair — flying DC8's.

When he left his Meteor over Derbyshire that December night, the aircraft plunged down into a plantation on Hagg Side, causing a deep crater. Although much of it was cleared, pieces of impacted metal and armour plating along with instrument cables and wires, remain in the crater at the wreck site.

Heavily compacted metal indicating the force with which the aircraft hit the ground.

Consul TF-RPM on delivery to an Icelandic airline, crashed on Crow Stone Edge, April 12, 1951. Map reference 177966.

A lone hiker, Mr. Ronald Yates of Pitsmoor, Sheffield was walking across Crow Stone Edge on Howden Moors when he caught sight of an aircraft fuselage and tail rearing up in the air. He discovered in the wreckage the bodies of three men — they appeared to have been killed instantly.

On the morning of April 12, 1951 Consul TF-RPM took off from Croydon headed for Iceland via Liverpool and Prestwick.

Built in 1942 by Airspeeds at Portsmouth, the Consul had begun its life as Oxford HN471, a trainer with the RAF. After the war it was re-purchased by Airspeed and underwent a conversion to a light civil transport. It was fitted out to carry six passengers; extra windows were installed, double doors were fitted to cut off the cockpit area and luggage space provided in an elongated nose. In its Airspeed livery of dark blue and gold it was purchased by an Icelandic airline company for around £5,500 and was on its delivery flight.

The pilot, Pall Magnusson aged 26 of Sentiarnarnesi, Iceland, had received a weather report from the Meteorological Office suggesting winds of up to 60 mph; that conditions were unfavourable for visual flying.

However, rather than use instruments, Magnusson opted for visual flying, which in effect meant keeping in sight of the ground and map-reading. Over the Pennines, in the area of the Dark Peak a near gale was blowing.

Acting as wireless operator was an Englishman, Alexander Watson aged 42 of Leytonstone, London. Watson was on loan to the Icelandic air company from Morton Air Services Ltd., of Croydon.

Flying as passenger was another Icelander, Johann Rist aged 35.

The crash site on Crow Stone Edge is 1,600 feet above sea level and is forty miles east of the planned course. A senior investigator of the Ministry of Aviation, Accident Investigation Branch, who examined the aircraft at the site, reported that in his opinion there had been no structural failure or mechanical breakdown prior to the crash. He also condidered that the plane had dived into the ground with both engines working under considerable power. As the pilot had not requested a change from visual to instrument flying — nor had there been any distress calls from the Consul, it would seem that the Icelander pilot had fallen into the same trap that other pilots had when flying over northern England.

The Consul would have started out safely flying under the clouds and then with the steadily rising ground would have been forced to climb above the overcast. The pilot would have been flying blind, having opted to travel by visual contact with the ground. Once he had assessed that they were clear of the hills he would have attempted to let down through the clouds in order to establish their position. High winds of up to 70 mph had pushed them into the heart of the Peak District where clouds and ground all too often meet.

Via WINTERBOTTOM

Vampire DH100, of R.A.F. North Luffenham crash-landed on Moscar Top, 300 yards from the Strines Inn, July 25, 1951. The pilot, Flying Officer Beckford escaped unhurt when the aircraft burst into flames.
Map reference 218899.

VIA BRIAN THIRKELL

Wellington MF 627, 6 Advanced Navigation School, on a cross country exercise from RAF Lichfield, crashed Ughill, October 17, 1952. Map reference 255896.

Take off time was 11.55; at the controls was Sergeant Reginald Keith and navigating was Pilot Officer David Ward, with Pilot Officer Brian Thirkell as second navigator.

After three hours the flight was nearing its end and Sergeant Keith was in contact with Lichfield and was entering the circuit prior to landing. The ground was obscured by low cloud and fog, so the approach was being made on the Gee homing system. In accord with normal procedure, the pilot asked the second navigator to "come up front" to be a second pair of eyes and to assist if necessary.

Brian Thirkell moved up into the cockpit, sat in the engineer's seat and fastened the six inch wide canvas safety strap across his chest. He recalls what happened next:

"I remember Sergeant Keith saying to me, "Look out for the ground." We were so confident of our position in relation to Lichfield that the undercarriage was down and the flaps partially lowered.

"Both of us saw the ground at the same time as it seemed to rush past just under the aircraft. The pilot rammed on the power; I reached out grabbed the throttle levers and held them. Sergeant Keith pulled back hard on the control column and we ploughed into the ground in an upward slide.

"Coming to rest the pilot and I clambered out through the roof of the cockpit virtually unharmed and surveyed the scene. "We were on quite a slope surrounded by swirling mist and under observation by some puzzled sheep. The tail section, still upright, had come to rest some distance from the main wreckage. One engine had rolled off down the hill and the fuselage aft of the main spar was split wide open.

"From within the shattered aircraft we could hear the moans of David Ward, so we scrambled in to get him. We carried him out and placed him on the upturned dinghy, which had self inflated upon impact — he was semi conscious."

Thirkell stayed with Ward whilst Keith went off for help, following some overhead cables. Some time later Keith returned with a farmer and contingents from the fire and ambulance brigades.

Wellington MF 627 had crashed fifty miles north of where the crew thought they were. The subsequent inquiry did not hold either navigators responsible, as they were not considered qualified. That left Sergeant Keith, as pilot in command and as the only qualified aircrew member he was held responsible for the loss of the aircraft. As it happened there were no serious injuries to the three crew members.

ASHTON-U-LYNE REPORTER

Beaver L-20, 26145 U.S.A.F. flying from Sculthorpe, Norfolk, to Burtonwood, crashed in mist on Bramah Edge, 12.30 p.m., December 5, 1956 killing the two American crew. Map reference 058978.

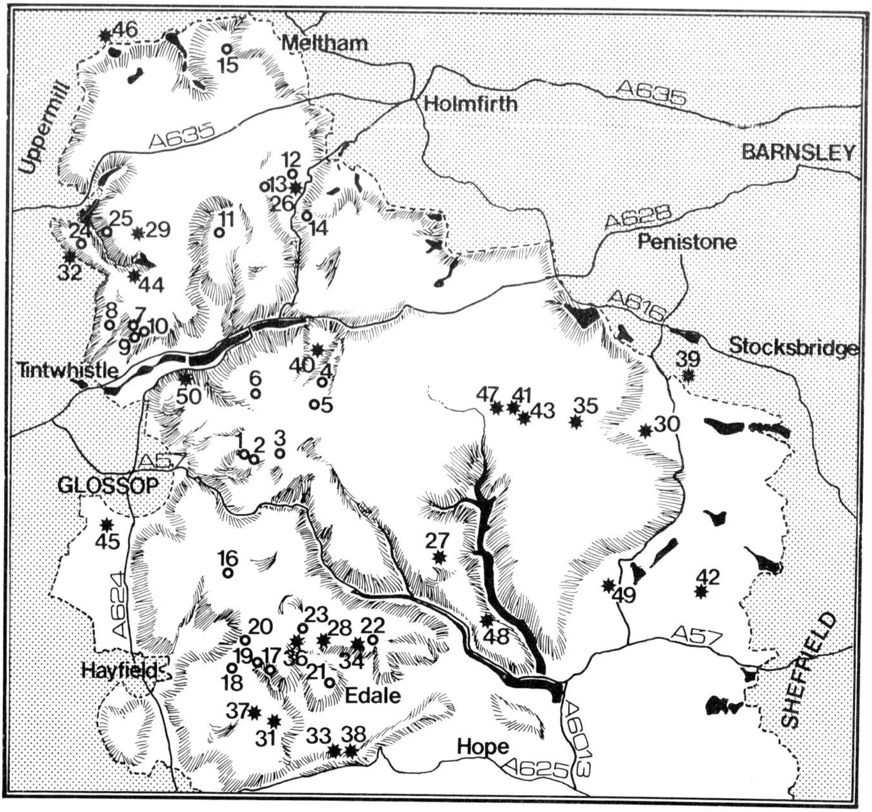

Crash sites covered in previous publication "Dark Peak Wrecks".

1 LANCASTER KB993
2 C-47 SKYTRAIN
3 SUPERFORTRESS
4 BOTHA
5 DEFIANT
6 BLENHEIM
7 LANCASTER PA411
8 CHIPMUNK
9 HURRICANES
10 LIGHTNING P38
11 METEORS
12 SABRE RCAF
13 SWORDFISH
14 LIBERATOR
15 FLYING FORTRESS
16 SABRES
17 ANSON LN185
18 HAWK
19 HARVARD
20 HAMPDEN
21 HEYFORD
22 WELLINGTON
23 RAPIDE
24 DAKOTA G-AHCY
25 MOSQUITO

Crash sites covered in this publication

26 HAMPDEN
27 DEFIANT
28 WELLINGTON W5719
29 LYSANDER
30 WELLINGTON DV810
31 THUNDERBOLT
32 PB4Y
33 SPITFIRE
34 HALIFAX
35 STIRLING
36 ANSON N9853
37 OXFORD HN594
38 OXFORD NM683
39 ANSON N9912
40 WELLINGTON R1011
41 OXFORD LX518
42 WELLINGTON MF627
43 BOMB
44 TIGER MOTH
45 MUSTANG
46 BARRACUDA
47 CONSUL
48 METEOR
49 VAMPIRE
50 BEAVER

Mountain Rescue Service

In the spring of 1943 the Air Ministry received a letter from the USAAF thanking them for the aid given to the pilot of one of their aircraft by the RAF Mountain Rescue Service, when the pilot had crashed in the Peak District. A nice gesture by the Americans, but the Air Ministry didn't know what their Allies were talking about! They had no such units known as "Mountain Rescue".

This well illustrates the situation surrounding the origins of the MRS. Rather than the powers of the Air Ministry directing, organising and equipping a rescue service to operate in the more desolate regions of this country to attend crashed aircraft, it was more a case of events forcing the birth of such a unit.

This story of mountain rescue in the Peak District began with 28 Maintenance Unit, based at Harpur Hill, Buxton and its Medical Officer, the then Flight Lieutenant David Crichton.

Back in 1942 calls became more frequent to Harpur Hill from police and farmers concerning aircraft crashes in their areas. "Doc" Crichton and a couple of RAF medical orderlies would turn out to give what assistance they could, with one small ambulance.

Specialised equipment was unheard of and the "doc" had to make do with the basics. As conditions in the hills grew more difficult, he was compelled to look around for help when a crash call came through; and volunteer helpers were drawn from any odd airmen who might be available at such a time.

Those who were prepared to be on call grew into a small band of volunteers, made up of tradesmen and technicians from all sorts of trades and crafts. When a call went out that an aircraft had crashed on the hills, they would set out and search together even at the end of a hard day's work, and then be on duty again in the morning after a night out on a rescue job.

"They were indeed a wonderful lot of chaps," Doc Crichton recalls. "We had no formal training, no special equipment and certainly no knowledge of mountaineering, so we had to do everything the hard way. Officially, as far as the Air Ministry was concerned, we did not exist."

"I remember going down to an old retired

sailor in Buxton who taught me how to splice ropes!"

Experience dictated the equipment needed — and the methods by which that essential equipment was acquired was better not examined too closely!

Similar RAF units in mountainous regions of this country — such as the one at Llandwrog in North Wales — were being forced into existence by sheer necessity.

By the end of 1943, the number of Allied airmen who had lost their lives in crashes on high ground in the United Kingdom had risen to a staggering 571. The Air Ministry was convinced.

The hitherto haphazard rescue arrangements were promptly organised and in January 1944, the RAF Mountain Rescue Service came into existence, officially.

Specialist equipment and training became available for the volunteers. By the end of 1944 eight teams were in existence and had attended 54 crashes, rescuing 49 airmen out of the 226 involved.

The Mountain Rescue Service Unit based at Harpur Hill, by the time of their official recognition had attended about 40 crashes. By dubious means they had "won" a Jeep, cold weather clothing, stronger boots than normal issue, a rocket gun and walkie-talkie sets.

Some necessary equipment was designed and manufactured on the spot by the volunteers themselves. They had discovered, for example, how difficult it was to transport casualties down cliffs and up steep slopes with ordinary stretchers, so a sledge was designed and built.

In those early days there were hardships and dangers for the volunteers, not just from extreme weather conditions experienced on the high ground but also from the crashed aircraft. Doc Crichton recalls "We must have been extraordinarily lucky not to have been injured ourselves while extracting casualties from the wrecks. Amongst the twisted metal we encountered bombs, ammunition and leaking high octane fuel!"

Doc Crichton, a pioneer of mountain rescue, left the MRS at Harpur Hill in 1946 and eventually retired from the RAF with the rank of Air Commodore. His place at Buxton was taken by Flight Lieutenant "Doc" McPherson, followed in turn by Squadron Leader Allen. From 1949 to 1952 Flight Lieutenant Fitton was in command.

It was during that imediate post-war period that much was done to improve the Service. More sophisticated equipment was provided and training courses in rock climbing, winter mountaineering and rescue were introduced for potential team leaders and members.

The Mountain Rescue Service has now been in existence for over forty years and although the incidence of air crashes has been virtually eliminated by better aviation equipment, and safety precautions, walkers still go missing on the moors, climbers are still injured and blizzards can and do still trap people on the roads over the high ground.

The MRS — born out of a need in the war years — still has a big part to play in the present day in the saving of human lives.

Acknowledgments

To produce a work of this nature demands the co-operation of many people. As it is a recording and collation of facts on a subject not treated in this way before, the need for accuracy has been closely borne in mind — so that history may not be abused.

The following names are those individuals who have kindly contributed in some way to this record — whether by the loan of photographs, supply of information, or giving of their time in other ways.

Without doubt, Mr. Collier could not begin his acknowledgment without first mentioning his wife Susan. Susan, it must be said, has not the slightest interest in aeroplanes — and when it comes to aircraft archaeology she does not know an oleo leg from a radial engine; this has not, however, prevented her from supporting Ron in his work. This has meant helping at exhibitions and lectures staged by him and has also included playing hostess to numerous aircraft wreck survivors who have revisited the area for the purpose of being interviewed. All this when Susan's own interests include pottery and hand painting of china, a far cry from the aviation relics which occupy so much of her husband's time and energies.

Some of the individuals and organisations who have made this work possible are as follows:

E. Acton, ex-Army Bomb Disposal. Air Data Publications. T. Allonby, aviation historian. K. Bancroft. S. Bishop, USAAF historian. Mrs. P. Buckley. V. Burk, 3rd Air Force historian. H. Cartwright, ex 150 Squadron. Miss E. Carter. J. Chappell, Holmfirth. ATC. P. Connatty, Loss lists and initial information. Captain Coyle, 427 Squadron historian. Mrs. Coulson, Canada. Air Commodore Crichton, doctor Mountain Rescue Service, retired. J. Davies, retired railwayman, Crowden. R. Freeman, 8th Air Force historian. D. Frith, historian. G. Graham, ex 150 Squadron. J. Hamer, ex searchlight unit, Edale, Mrs. F. Herdman, Edale. H. Holmes, 8th Air Force historian. R. Ives, aviation historian. J. Mason, gamekeeper. W. Matthews, New Zealand. K. Merrick, author. M. Oates, Edale. J. O'Connell, ex police special constable, Meltham. J. Ownsworth, aviation historian. J. Price, ex 150 Squadron. Mrs. P. Quill, New Zealand. I. Reynolds, ex 427 Squadron, Canada. B. Robinson, archivist. W. Russell, USA. P. Shaw, mountain rescue team. L. Sidwell, 7 Squadron historian. D. Smith aviation historian/author. B. Stevens, aviation historian. A. Stovell, C. Sutcliffe, Ashton-under-Lyne Reporter. F. Tasker, Meltham. Bernard Taylor, retired schoolteacher. J. Townsend, ex-gamekeeper. W. Utton, Mossley. Air Commodore Wake, ex 166 Squadron. H. Ward, ex radio operator, Ringway. A. Weldon, ex 150 Squadron. ACCIDENT INVESTIGATION BRANCH, DEPARTMENT OF TRADE, V. G. S. Caseley. 28 MAINTENANCE UNIT MOUNTAIN RESCUE TEAM, C. Austin; Squadron Leader K. Fitton; S. Heywood; W. Parks; D. Pritchard. MOD, NAVAL HISTORICAL BRANCH, J. Brown. PUBLIC RECORDS OFFICE, F. F. Lambert. POLISH AIR FORCE ASSOCIATION, 2ND AIR DIVISION NEWSLETTER, W. Robertie, Editor. AIR FORCE RELATIONS OFFICER, ROYAL NEW ZEALAND AIR FORCE, Squadron Leader K. Lumsden. 1196 SQUADRON A.T.C. OFFICERS, STAFF AND CADETS 1965-1979. DIRECTOR AND STAFF OF: CASUALTY BRANCH; OFFICES RECORDS; AIRMEN RECORDS; AUSTRALIAN RECORDS; CANADIAN RECORDS. Mr. E. H. Turner and Staff of 'AHB' MOD. Ted Hines, IWM. Joan Padley, secretary and typist.

KEN KERSHAW, Ron Collier's walking companion — who originally suggested the idea of a book on the subject; mention must be made too, of the friends who acted as companions and guides to the crash sites: NORMAN WINTERBOTTOM, GERALD SCARRETT, and all the members of GLOSSOP and PEAK DISTRICT AIRCRAFT ARCHAEOLOGY SOCIETY.

THE FEATURES AND GRAPHICS DEPARTMENT OF THE BARNSLEY CHRONICLE herewith acknowledge help and assistance provided by the following persons: QUENTIN GRAY, Managing Editor, Huddersfield District Newspapers (1975) Limited, who first published the series "Dark Peak Wrecks"; PAT GWYNNETTE, typist; ARTHUR WATSON, Keyboard operator; JOHN FAWCETT and NICHOLAS GILLOTT, Process consultants; FRANK NEWMAN, ex-Halifax flight engineer; BRYAN COX, who aided in crash site location.

MINISTRY OF DEFENCE
AIR FORCE BOARD SECRETARIAT
CRASHED MILITARY AIRCRAFT OF HISTORICAL INTEREST
NOTE OF GUIDANCE TO RECOVERY GROUPS

1. One result of the growing public interest in the history of aviation, and the Second World War in particular, is that a number of groups have been formed to recover, preserve and exhibit some of the military aircraft which crashed during the war and have never been recovered. The level of activity is such that it is considered necessary to issue this Note of Guidance on matters which are of particular concern to the Ministry of Defence.

Ownership of aircraft and equipment and retention of recovered items.

2. Crashed British military aircraft and their equipment **remain the property of the Ministry of Defence until such time as the Crown decides to dispose of them** (see para 4 below). Crashed enemy aircraft and their equipment lying within the United Kingdom are regarded as captured enemy property which has been surrendered to the Crown. For all practical purposes the Ministry of Defence can exercise the right to possession of both categories and deal with any question arising on them. Should the Royal Air Force undertake any of the recovery work in connection with human remains (see para 10), any additional non-prohibited items thereby recovered will be offered to the group concerned.

Permission to recover

3. Any recovery group wishing to recover the wreckage of a military aircraft should first approach the Ministry of Defence to obtain their consent as owner. Consent will normally be given, subject to the various requirements contained in this Note and to the condition that the work will be carried out in a responsible manner. Consent may be withheld, however, in cases where the Ministry of Defence wishes to make its own arrangements for the recovery and/or preservation of an aircraft. Consent must be obtained with respect to each and every recovery operation, and groups should note that the Ministry of Defence is not prepared to grant sole rights of recovery to any one group for any one site.

4. The Ministry of Defence requires to know what items have been recovered by groups who have been granted permission to recover crashed military aircraft. A report is to be rendered on a special proforma and returned to the Ministry of Defence at the address shown in para 16 below when the project is completed. Recovery groups will then receive, in due course, formal written notification from the Ministry of Defence that the items listed on the proforma may be regarded as their own property. Until such time as they have been notified however, recovery groups are reminded that the items **remain the property of the Crown** and are not to be considered their own.

5. Any failure to follow the guidance given in this Note will result in a recovery becoming an unlawful interference with Crown property and could lead to civil or criminal proceedings. In this respect particular attention is drawn to para 9 concerning firearms, ammunition and explosives, and para 10 concerning human remains.

Entry on to land

6. In all cases the permission of landowners and occupiers should be obtained before any recovery project is undertaken. Once permission has been granted, full liaison should be maintained with the landowner or occupier in order to ensure the minimum of inconvenience and damage to property.

Wreckage lying in coastal waters

7. Groups wishing to recover aircraft lying in coastal waters are advised that, in addition to approaching the Ministry of Defence, as laid down in this Note, they must also contact the local Receiver of Wreck, who is ultimately responsible for determining the ownership of any such aircraft.

Safety precautions

8. Recovery operations should not commence until adequate safety precautions, commensurate with the dangers likely to be encountered, have been taken. For example, if an aircraft lies on a former bombing or gunnery range, or if the presence of any firearms, ammunition or explosives is suspected, expert advice should be sought from the police or any Service unit. (See also paragragh 9).

Firearms, ammunition and explosives

9. The possession of firearms, ammunition and explosives is subject to strict control under the Firearms Act 1968 and the Explosives Act 1875, and any person having unauthorised possession of them would commit an offence. The finding of firearms, ammunition and explosives should be notified immediately to the police. This applies in all cases irrespective of the condition of the items found, and recovery work is to cease until the items have been removed by properly authorised persons and the site declared safe. The Ministry of Defence specifically reserves its rights of ownership in respect of prohibited weapons and ammunition (whatever the condition) detailed under Section 5 of the Firearms Act 1968, that is, any firearm designed or adapted for continuous fire or for the discharge of any noxious liquid, gas etc. and any ammunition containing or designed or adapted to contain any such noxious thing. The retention of any firearm or ammunition under Section 1 of the Firearms Act 1968 is, of course, subject to the possession of a Firearm Certificate.

Human remains

10. In many cases crews will have escaped from aircraft before they crashed, but there is still a possibility of human remains being found. These must not be touched and they should be treated with due respect. Their discovery must be reported immediately to the police and the Ministry of Defence, AR9(RAF), Adastral House, Theobalds Road, London WC1X 8RU, Tel. 01-430 7577. Recovery activities must be suspended and nothing should be taken from the site until both the Royal Air Force and the police have made their investigations and the human remains have been removed. The feelings of relatives of deceased aircrew cannot be emphasised too strongly. Irreverent handling of human remains would be particularly distressing to them and it is most important that no information about the discovery of human remains should be given to presumed relatives or the news media, or indeed to anyone outside the police or the Ministry of Defence, until the facts have been properly confirmed. A coroner's inquest may have to be held. The Ministry of Defence will take all necessary steps to notify the next-of-kin or other relatives, and in no circumstances is a recovery group to act in this respect.

Personal property

11. Items might be found in wreckage which were the personal property of crew members. These must be handed to the police or any Service unit.

Books, documents and papers

12. All books, documents and papers found during excavation, whether official or personal crew property, must be reported to the Ministry of Defence, who will then decide which items, if any, may be retained by the group in question.

Legal responsibilities

13. It must be clearly understood that the Ministry of Defence will not under any circumstances accept any responsibility whatsoever for any consequences arising from the activities of recovery groups, for example compensation for injury to any persons or damage to any property. This Note is not therefore to be construed as an authority from the Ministry of Defence to recover aircraft, but rather as a guide to the circumstances under which the Ministry of Defence may consent to an application for recovery. Groups are urged to consider their position before embarking upon a project.

Adverse publicity

14. The Ministry of Defence is concerned that the Services should not become involved in any adverse publicity as the result of any recovery activities. Groups are requested to take all possible steps to prevent this.

US military aircraft

15. Any enquiries concerning the investigation or recovery of US military aircraft of historical interest are to be directed to the Ministry of Defence, who will act on behalf of the US authorities.

Reports, applications and enquiries

16. Reports of items recovered (see para 4 above) and any applications or enquiries regarding recovery operations covered by this Note should be addressed to:

Ministry of Defence, Air Force Board Secretariat, Room 8239, Main Building, Whitehall, SW1A 2HB.